30 Minute Vegeta

30 Minute Vegetarian Italian Cookbook

Marlena Spieler

Thorsons
An Imprint of HarperCollins*Publishers*

Thorsons
An Imprint of HarperCollins*Publishers*
77–85 Fulham Palace Road
Hammersmith, London W6 8JB

Published by Thorsons 1998
1 3 5 7 9 10 8 6 4 2

A catalogue record for this book is available
from the British Library

ISBN 0 7225 3648 8

Printed and bound in Great Britain by
Caledonian International Book Manufacturing Ltd, Glasgow

Contents

Acknowledgements

Grazie bene: to Leah for falling in love with Roma as a little girl; Jon for falling in love with Leah. To Alan who is very brave, and to Gretchen, who is even braver – considering the travels I've roped her into.

To my literary/media agent and e-mail pal, Borra Garson; M.A. Mariner, Fran Irwin and her feline family; all of my colleagues at the *San Francisco Chronicle*; *Bon Appetit* magazine for sending me into the kitchen on a fennel foray; Sue Kreitzman, not only for being a friend, but also for her inspiring low-fat cuisine; Sri and Roger Owen who are magnificent hosts and Italophiles extraordinaire; Philippa Davenport; Michele Turney for her careful, thoughtful editing.

To friends in tasting: Dr Esther Novak and Revd John Chendo; Rabbi Jason Gaber; Mary and Fred Barclay; Sandy Waks; Kamala Friedman; Nigel Patrick; Graham Ketteringham; Paula Levine and family; Paul Richardson for sharing Sardinia; and Amanda Hamilton and Tim Hemmeter for sharing their vineyard in Sonoma, California; Jerome Freeman and Sheila Hannon who sometimes know me as 'Mama Rosa'.

Grazie also to: Lynne Meikle at Tate and Lyle for her sugar expertise and knowledge; Fortnum and Mason for the most exquisite of dried mushrooms and their wonderful selection of olive oils and other delicacies *Italiano*; Thomas and Thomas for their dried mushrooms; Harvey Nichols for olive oil and dried mushrooms; Dr Stefano Raimundo and the Italian Trade

Commission; Caroline Black at Grayling PR (European Olive Oil Commission); Anne Dolomore and Judy Ridgway for olive oil expertise; Leon Frenkl Olive Oil Importing (Lanfranci); Panayis Manuelides and Alice Seferiades of Odysea Imports; Elaine Ashton (Grania and Sarnia) for her fantastic southern Italian imports: olive oil, quail egg pasta, truffle paste extraordinaire; Gianni and Pamela Parmigiani (the quality of whose olive oil is equalled only by their luscious Parmesan cheese); Priscilla Carluccio (Carluccios); David Roberts and Paolo Ardisson of John Burgess Exports; Charles Carey of Donatantonio PLC; Crispin Burridge of Marks and Spencer for a behind-the-scenes tour of northern Italy's yummiest *biscotti* and *pasticcerie*; Schwartz Spices for adding fragrance and flavour to my Italian kitchen; Le Creuset pots and saucepans – especially their excellent ridged grillpan – for making everything seem to cook so effortlessly.

A la famiglia: my parents, Caroline and Izzy Smith; grandmother, Sophia Dubowsky; aunt and uncle, Estelle and Sy Opper; and my little cousins, Melissa, Steven, Alison, Lexie, and Jordan.

Introduction

Ah, Italy. Where else can a vegetarian eat so happily, so easily, so sensually and so quickly, too? The foods of Italy are fresh and invigorating, a pleasure for all who love vegetables.

The Italian passion for good food is legendary: they love to eat well – healthily and pleasurably – several times a day. Most people, though, live busy lives, juggling their career commitments with home, family and social life. Few Italians are able to spend all day cooking, any more than those of us in northern Europe or America are able to.

But in Italy, where quality is superb, it is the simple foods that are the best: boiled potatoes glistening with olive oil, slices of smoky grilled aubergine, wedges of egg-rich frittata, plates of tomatoey pasta abundant with the freshest of vegetables, and little leafy salads, all eaten with a chunk of bread to mop up the delicious juices. Meals like this take scarcely minutes to toss together. *La cucina rapida*, the art of quickly-prepared meals, is thus as much a fixture in the Italian kitchen as it is in ours.

Italian cooks are indeed privileged with their choice of ingredients: fragrant olive oil, chewy or tender pastas, pungent cheeses, honest bread tasting of wheat, tangy olives, and always the freshest of vegetables, salads, herbs and fruit.

Visit any village or city market and what you find is strictly in season, fresh and intensely flavoured. The decision of what to cook is usually made on the spot at the market: what is the nicest, the freshest and, of course, the most reasonably priced? Many people in Italy have a tiny garden, even if only a few tomato plants on the side of the road, or little pots of basil, parsley, rosemary and other herbs growing on the terrace of a city apartment.

Italian food is still guided by tradition but has opened its doors to other influences, too. While regional specialities are still a great delight, many such dishes have migrated from north to south or vice versa. And some dishes, such as the Neopolitan pizza, have claimed Italy entirely, then taken on the entire world.

The traditional structure of an Italian meal usually consists of appetizers/*antipasti*, such as mixed vegetable dishes, or a first course (*primo piatto*), such as pasta or soup, though many impassioned Italian eaters like to include both. *Antipasti* consists of a tangy vegetable concoction, or perhaps a wedge of frittata, a crisp little pizza, a plate of olives and celery, vegetables with an olive oil dip, or garlicky bruschetta. One of the most enticing sights in Italy is the *antipasto* table: a wide array of plates or bowls filled with salads, marinated vegetables, crostini, etc. (though some of the dishes are not vegetarian, many are).

The first course after the *antipasti* is usually pasta, soup or risotto. Pasta is the most convenient of foods: waiting almost indefinitely on the store cupboard shelf, needing only to be combined with a simple sauce or splash of olive oil and whatever vegetables are freshest in the market or garden. Throughout the book I have used the term *al dente* when referring to cooking pasta. This literally means 'to the tooth', describing the way perfectly cooked pasta should be – just slightly resistant to the tooth as you bite in, then yielding itself as you chew. Risottos – rice-based dishes – are convenient too, and Italian soups can be surprisingly light, vivacious and quick to prepare.

The main course that follows might be animal-based, but vegetarians can opt for a pasta or risotto, or a big hefty soup. Grilled vegetables, hefty stews and sautées of sun-drenched vegetables are also good choices.

The south, long an impoverished region, has traditionally sustained itself on vegetables, pastas and beans. Further north, Tuscany is justly famous for its beans, bread-based dishes and barbecued whole porcini mushrooms, a delicacy when mushrooms are in season.

But a meal *al Italiana* does not need to follow the traditional pattern. It can just as easily be a one-course wonder: a bowl of hearty soup, a savoury pizza or frittata, accompanied by a fresh and crisp little salad. End the meal with a short, strong espresso, a tiny thimble of pure, dark coffee flavour – never the milky cappuccino, for the latter is too filling after a meal. Nibble on a piece of exquisitely fresh fruit: a wedge of melon, a juicy pear, or bowl of cherries cooled with a handful of ice cubes rather than in the refrigerator.

Regardless of their lack of time, no Italian wants to forgo the pleasures – both socially and gastronomically – of the table and the wellbeing that good food imparts to us all. Nor should you. The following collection of authentic Italian dishes can be prepared in 30 minutes or fewer; some will leave you enough time for a nice glass of wine, and a chance to put your feet up, too.

Buon Appetito!

La Dispensa/
The Store Cupboard

A store cupboard of good Italian ingredients is vital for the 30-minute cook – the olive oil, dried mushrooms, herbs and flavourings impart the distinctive and delicious character of the Italian peninsula. In this section is a list and description of what I suggest keeping to hand.

Shopping for Italian ingredients is fun: the aromas, the beautiful green-gold bottles of olive oil, the sachets of dried mushrooms, the pots of brightly coloured pastes – olive, tomato, artichoke, basil. A visit to an Italian deli is almost as pleasant as a trip to Italy, such is the appeal of the ingredients. Supermarkets, too, stock a wide assortment of Italian ingredients these days. For a list of recommended suppliers, *see Resources, page 203.*

Beans and Lentils

With their sustaining protein and satisfying heft, beans and lentils are a boon to vegetarians. They are also a staple in the Italian diet. While dried beans take a long time to cook – several hours, not counting the soaking time – they are readily available, and very good, in tins: choose borlotti, red kidney, chickpeas, cannellini and brown lentils. When using tinned beans, rinse in cold water first to rid them of their salty flavour.

Another way of having cooked beans available when you are ready to cook is to make a big pot of beans and freeze them in portions. Defrost by leaving them out in the morning or – as I find very convenient – in the microwave. I might not recommend the microwave for a great deal of cooking (with the terrific exception of risotto), but for defrosting, it is a great help.

Capers

Capers come from the buds of the caper plant that grows wild throughout the Mediterranean. The best capers to my mind are from the Italian island of Pantellaria – big, fat, flavourful things preserved in salt rather than vinegar. Capers add a particular and distinctive flavour, and shouldn't be abused. Many feel that capers are an acquired taste. I feel that it is a taste well worth acquiring for the added punch and zest the little buds can add to foods such as pizza, pasta and *antipasti*.

Cheeses

(For Parmesan and other grating cheeses, *see Parmesan*.)
Gorgonzola, a creamy, blue-veined cheese from the region of Lombardy, is full of rich flavour and can be quite pungent as well. Ricotta is made from whey. It is like a curdless cottage cheese, delicious eaten either savoury, spooned onto pasta, or sweetened with sugar and flavourings for dessert. Bel Paese is a nice dessert cheese, so too is stracchino – pungent, runny and irresistible. Fontina is mild, creamy and deliciously meltable. The finest is from Italy, but Danish fontina can be used at a pinch.

Mozzarella is best eaten fresh. The finest is made from buffalo milk in the area just north of Naples: it is milky, fresh and very perishable. True *aficionados* judge the age of mozzarella by hours rather than days. Firm mozzarella is not as enchanting as moist, fresh mozzarella, but is at its best sliced and melted over pizza and other baked dishes.

Dried Mushrooms

Dried mushrooms add the flavour and aroma of the woods to a huge variety of foods in the Italian kitchen. The most famous is the porcini, a fragrant fungus that grows under the chestnut tree and adds its distinctive flavour to pasta, soups and risottos. Porcini are expensive but pack a huge flavour wallop, so you only need to use a small amount. I have found Argentinean porcini imported to California that cost a fraction of the price, and may soon be available in the UK too.

Frozen Vegetables

Some frozen vegetables are convenient to keep on hand. Frozen peas, artichoke hearts, sweetcorn and spinach are in my freezer most of the time; other vegetables I find less satisfactory.

Garlic

The stinking rose of garlic, that fragrant, deliciously reeking bulb, so beloved throughout the Mediterranean. Most Italians, especially from the dignified and refined north, use far less garlic than I do. I can seldom be restrained when it comes to adding garlic.

Herbs – Dried

Stock up on oregano leaves, mixed Italian herbs, fennel seeds, thyme and marjoram. I do keep dried basil, though I find it good for only one or two dishes, and prefer the fresh for almost everything.

Herbs – Fresh

Try if you can to keep several pots of herbs growing on your windowsill: fresh basil, rosemary, sage, parsley (flat leaf), mint, oregano or marjoram.

Olives

Taste your way through your local delicatessen for the olives you like best. Gaeta olives – rich, black and full of flavour – are excellent with Italian dishes; so, too, are many of the oil-cured or salt-cured black olives from elsewhere.

Olive Oil

A drizzle of extra virgin olive oil gives the flavour of Italy not only to Mediterranean vegetables and salads, but also to such humble foods as boiled potatoes, beetroot, carrots, spinach and cabbage greens. Olive oil is a complete spectrum of flavour nuances, aromas, colours and quality. You will need to taste your way through the peppery Tuscans and the gutsy Abruzzi, the fragrant Molise and feisty Sicilian, the light and fragrant Ligurian

...Umbria, Puglia...each region produces oils with different characteristics. The wealth of variety is endless, so do keep a few favourites on hand.

To store olive oil, keep it in a green glass bottle with a tightly sealed top, and place it in a cool, dark place. Don't refrigerate it as it solidifies when chilled. Once opened, oil should keep for about two to three months. Unopened, it should keep for up to about a year.

Parmesan

Good quality Parmesan – *Parmigiano-Reggiano* – is one of the most delicious of cheeses, not just for grating where it imparts its distinguished zest, but also for nibbling on after dinner with a ripe pear or a few persimmons (sharon fruit), or simply for grabbing as a snack. A good *Parmigiano* is the yellow of straw, crumbly but still moist, and bursting with flavour. Buy it in chunks and grate it as needed. Wrap the *Parmigiano* in foil and store it in the refrigerator. Other good cheeses for grating include pecorino, with its tang of the barnyard; grana padano; and, if you live in California, dried Monterey Jack. Do not use pre-grated Parmesan cheese; to me, it is disgusting and spoils all it is added to.

Passata

Pure liquefied tomatoes, usually sold in cardboard containers or glass bottles, passata makes a terrific basis for pasta and pizza sauces, or to pour into soups.

Pasta

The wide variety of pasta available can make every meal an adventure. Always keep a few different types of pasta on your shelves: a few chunky shapes, a few long strands, and one or two small pastas or *pastine* for soups.

Pickles and Preserved Vegetables

Keep supplies of roasted peppers, artichoke paste, artichoke hearts in marinade, aubergines (eggplants) (roasted, in marinade, and as a purée), olive (green and black) paste, pesto (some brands are better than others), sun-dried tomatoes in marinade or in paste.

You can roast peppers by placing the whole peppers directly on top of a barbecue or arranging them on a baking sheet under the grill. Cook on a medium-high heat until they are lightly and evenly blistered and charred. Place them in a plastic bag or a bowl and seal tightly. Leave for at least 30 minutes. Remove and peel. The skin should slip off fairly easily. Save the juices as desired. Discard stem, seeds and skin and use the pepper flesh as you like.

Pizza Bases

Commercially made pizza bases are of varying quality. You will probably need to try several different brands before you settle on one you like. Flour tortillas and focaccio bread are all good to use for DIY pizzas, too.

Polenta

Coarsely milled maize or corn, polenta is cooked into a golden-yellow gruel and eaten in soft billows topped with melting butter, cheese, savoury tomato sauces or sautéed wild mushrooms. Or it is poured onto a flat surface and left to cool, then eaten as bread, cooked over the grill alongside mushrooms or vegetables, or layered into casseroles and baked with tomatoes, cheeses and herbs. Polenta takes about 35–40 minutes of cooking and stirring, but instant polenta takes about six minutes. Though it lacks the hearty corn flavour one expects in polenta, it is still very good for layering and grilling, and even, if you love polenta as much as I do, on its own.

Rice

Keep a box of both long-grain rice for rice dishes such as Rice with Herbs, and Arborio or Carnaroli rice for risotto.

Stock

You will need a supply of good-quality vegetable stock, either fresh or frozen (which is increasingly available). In the US, tinned stock can be found as well. Stock cubes can be salty, but add a necessary flavour to risottos and soups. Italians occasionally toss a small amount of stock cube into a tomato sauce in place of salt to give a long-simmered flavour to a quick sauce.

Tinned Tomatoes

Usually sold as whole or diced, they range from anaemic to quite tasty. Some are packed with basil or other herbs, and some are better than others. I like the Valfrutta brand.

Tomato Purée

Thick and dark-red, tomato purée is essence of tomato cooked down to an intense and thick paste. In Italy's south you will also find very thick and dark tomato pastes called *estrattu*.

Truffle Oil

A rich and fragrant condiment that imparts the scent of truffles to all it touches. Sprinkle onto just-tender green beans, sautéed wild mushrooms, eggs baked with cream, or pasta with warm garlic butter or oil. You only need – indeed, it is so strong, you only *want* – a few drops at a time. You can also find truffle vinegar which gives a lighter, albeit earthy, fragrant touch to salads.

Vinegar

Red and white wine vinegar are indispensable in the Italian kitchen to add zing to salads, to sprinkle onto cooked vegetables, to sharpen sauces with a tangy drop. Balsamic vinegar is another addition to my Italian kitchen: a richly flavoured vinegar, aged long in wooden barrels, with a sweet and mellow rather than a sour tang. Balsamic vinegar is good tossed into salads with olive oil to balance the acidity of other vinegars; or dribble a few drops onto sweetened strawberries or into puréed soft fruit sauces.

Wine

The Italian kitchen is never without a bottle of wine, to sip as you stir your risotto, to tip a glass into the simmering soup, to stir a few ounces into your pasta sauce. For cooking simple, straight-forward food, as most Italian food is, gravitate towards the simple, even humble wines rather than anything serious or complex. Taste your way through Italy's offerings – most of the super-markets have well-defined labels that can help you choose. I've read and sipped my way, very successfully, through the wine sections at Tesco, Somerfield, Sainsbury, Marks and Spencer and KwikSave.

Antipasti
Appetizers

Antipasti – those nibbles that form the first course, sometimes instead of, other times in addition to, the starter – offer the essential flavour of Italy.

Antipasti literally means the meal before the meal. These sprightly and vivacious foods ease you into the meal and take the edge off the appetite but do not fill you up. The little selection of vegetables – raw and salad-like or cooked and cooled, perhaps a plate of olives and/or fresh mozzarella, with crusty bread to scoop up the morsels – is food meant to be savoured slowly, chatted over, enjoyed with a glass of wine or cooling water, a transition from the business of life to the enjoyment of the table.

Foods that make excellent *antipasti* can also be found in other chapters: pizzas, crostini and bruschette, as well as wedges of omelettes or frittata. For recipes and ideas, *see Chapter 7.*

Crisp-crumbed, Roasted Tomatoes

Each bite of *tomates al forno* is flavoured with the sun and is almost a mini-holiday in itself. Serve either warm or cool, with a few jet-black wrinkled olives alongside, and perhaps a glass of chilled rosé.

Leftovers of this dish are quite practical as well as tasty: dice up the tomatoes and delicious crumb stuffing and toss them into hot, freshly cooked spaghetti, dressed with olive oil and garlic.

SERVES 4

4 large or 8 small-to-medium	ripe and flavourful tomatoes
	salt to taste
3–5 cloves	garlic, chopped
60–90 g/2–3 oz/2–3 cups	fresh basil or 1–2 tsp fresh rosemary, chopped
4–5 tbsp	extra virgin olive oil
3 tbsp	each grated Parmesan (or pecorino) and fresh breadcrumbs

1) Cut the tomatoes into halves crosswise and lightly squeeze out the seeds and juices of each half; save this for soups and/or sauces. Sprinkle the cut sides with salt.

2) Crush the garlic then add the basil and about 60 ml/2 fl oz/¼ cup of the olive oil, then stuff the tomatoes with this mixture.

3) Mix the cheese and breadcrumbs then stuff the basil-filled tomatoes with this mixture and drizzle with the remaining olive oil. Place the tomatoes in a large baking pan, preferably a ceramic roasting pan.

4) Roast at 180–190°C/350–375°F/gas mark 4–6 for 20 minutes or until the tomatoes are lightly browned on top and tender inside.
5) Serve hot, or leave them to cool to room temperature and serve them as an appetizer with their juices slightly thickened and utterly delicious.

Ligurian Black Olive Paste

Black olive paste (olivada) – pungent, salty, tasting like essence of olives and herbs – is evocative of meals eaten along the Ligurian coast.

Serve it as an *antipasto*, spread onto thickly buttered little toasts topped with halves of hard-boiled egg, or sliced barbecued potatoes.

MAKES ABOUT 350 G/12 OZ

1 clove	garlic, crushed
4–6 tbsp	black olive paste
90 ml/3 fl oz/⅓ cup	extra virgin olive oil
1 tsp each:	herbs de Provence and fennel seeds
2 tbsp	chopped fresh rosemary

1) Combine the garlic with the olive paste, olive oil, dried herbs and fennel, and rosemary.

Spicy Brown Lentils

I generally use Puy lentils for lenticchie con aglio – although they aren't Italian, they have a lovely steely-grey colour and deep flavour, plus they hold their shape so well in cooking. To follow this *antipasto*, serve a dish of pasta with lots of vegetables that you can toss together while the lentils are simmering, say, Spaghettini with Asparagus and Capers (*see page 72*).

SERVES 4

175 g/6 oz/1 cup	brown lentils
3	bay leaves
350 ml/12 fl oz/1½ cups	water
	cayenne pepper or other chilli pepper flavouring
4–6 tbsp	olive oil
2 cloves	garlic, chopped
	salt to taste
1 tbsp	coarsely chopped flat-leaf parsley

1) Combine the lentils with the bay leaves and water and bring to the boil. Reduce the heat and cook over a medium heat for about 20 minutes. This is enough for most lentils to retain their shape and be tender but not mushy. If the mixture is too dry, add a little more water.
2) Drain, reserving the liquid for soups.
3) Dress the lentils in cayenne or other hot pepper, olive oil, garlic, salt and parsley. Serve warm.

Artichokes Sicilian-style

I like this so much that I often make a double batch and enjoy the leftovers at room temperature the next day as an *antipasto*. Mint and lemon are utterly refreshing with artichokes.

SERVES 4

4 medium-sized	artichokes
1	lemon, quartered
125 ml/4 fl oz/½ cup	extra virgin olive oil
4–5 cloves	garlic, thinly sliced or coarsely chopped
60 g/2 oz/4 cups	fresh mint, coarsely chopped
250 ml/8 fl oz/1 cup	dry white wine, such as Soave
250 ml/8 fl oz/1 cup	water, more if needed
	salt to taste

1) Quarter the artichokes. Cut off stems and trim stringy skins. With a teaspoon and a sharp paring knife, remove the inner choke and thistly inner bits. Place each quarter into a bowl of cold water into which you have squeezed one of the lemon quarters.
2) Dry the prepared artichokes with a clean towel and throw away the water they have been soaking in.
3) Heat the olive oil with half the garlic and mint, and in this brown the artichokes gently on all sides. When they are lightly browned, add the wine and water, salt to taste and the rest of the lemon, then cover and cook for 15–20 minutes or until just tender. Add the rest of the garlic and cook for another 5 minutes. If there is too much liquid, boil it down until it forms a concentrated, flavourful sauce. Serve warm or leave to cool.

Grapefruit with Campari

The bitter-sweet flavour of Campari enhances the tanginess of the grapefruit. This also makes a light and invigorating dessert.

SERVES 4

2–3 grapefruit, chilled

3–6 tbsp Campari, or as desired

1) Peel the grapefruit using a sharp paring knife, trimming off all the white pith. Cut the grapefruit into peeled segments by inserting your knife between the segment membranes and cutting nearly to the core on each side of a segment. A peeled segment of grapefruit will pop out of your fruit. Continue until all the grapefruit have been cut. Save the juices to pour over the grapefruit.

2) Arrange the segments on plates and drizzle with Campari. Serve.

Roasted Peppers with Goat's Cheese

This tangy *antipasto* offers a big jolt of Mediterranean flavour. Serve it to begin a meal of Pasta Arrabbiatta (*see page 79*) or Spaghetti Alla Norma (*see page 101*).

SERVES 4

1 jar	roasted red pepper, drained, or 2 red peppers roasted and peeled and cut into strips
4–6	marinated sun-dried tomatoes (in a jar) cut into thin strips (optional)
125 g/4 oz/1 cup	fresh, white, slightly salty cheese such as Pecorino, feta or goat's cheese, crumbled
1–2 cloves	garlic, chopped
2 tbsp	olive oil, or to taste
1 tsp	red wine vinegar, or to taste
2–3 tbsp	fresh basil leaves, thinly sliced or 1 tsp fresh marjoram, chopped
3 tbsp	pine kernels or flaked almonds

1) Lightly toast the pine kernels or almonds in a heavy, ungreased frying pan over a medium heat, tossing them every few moments. This should take only about 5 minutes. Remove from the pan and let them cool for a few moments.

2) Arrange the peppers on a plate, then garnish with the sun-dried tomatoes if using, then the cheese. Sprinkle with the garlic, dress with the olive oil and vinegar, then scatter the basil or marjoram and pine kernels or flaked almonds over the top. Serve right away or chill before serving.

Red Pepper Rolls Stuffed with Melted Cheese

I often add a spoonful of capers to the shredded cheese, as I love their briny, tangy flavour. Diced tomatoes, too, give a deliciously pizza-like quality.

SERVES 4

4	roasted red peppers, halved or quartered
175–250 g/6–8 oz/1½–2 cups	fontina cheese, coarsely shredded
3–5 tbsp	fresh basil, thinly sliced
2 cloves	garlic, chopped (optional)
drizzle of	olive oil

1) Heat the grill or the oven to 200°C/400°F/gas mark 6.
2) Lay the peppers flat and sprinkle first with cheese then with the basil and garlic (if using). Roll each up and secure with a skewer (or place seam-side down) and arrange in a baking dish. Drizzle with olive oil.
3) Bake or grill until the cheese melts and the peppers sizzle. Serve right away, taking care not to burn your tongue on the hot cheese.

Sweet-sour Antipasto of Beetroot

Splashing on a sweet-sour dressing can save even vinegar-dressed supermarket beetroot and make it delicious.

I might make a meal of various *antipasti*, including this one, and the cheese and salad topped piadine (*see Chapter 7, page 187*).

SERVES 4

4 medium-sized	cooked beetroot, peeled and sliced
3–5	shallots, chopped or ½ red onion, chopped
1–1½ tbsp	sugar, preferably lightly refined such as Demerara, or to taste
2–3 tbsp	red wine vinegar, or to taste

1) Arrange the beetroot on a plate, sprinkling it with the shallots as you layer it. Combine the sugar and red wine, then pour it over the beetroot and shallots evenly.

Antipasto of Grilled Vegetables and Pesto

Bits of grilled courgettes (zucchini) and sweet peppers, tossed with diced tomatoes and fragrant pesto tastes quintessentially of Meditteranean summer. Sometimes I serve this with a sprinkling of pine kernels, either raw or toasted, and an extra scattering of basil.

SERVES 4

4	courgettes (zucchini), sliced ¼-inch thick
1 red and 1 yellow	pepper, quartered
olive oil for drizzling	
½ tsp	balsamic vinegar, or to taste
2–3 cloves	garlic, chopped
	salt and pepper
4	ripe tomatoes, diced
4–6 tbsp	pesto

1) Arrange the courgette (zucchini) and pepper pieces on a baking dish and drizzle with olive oil and balsamic vinegar, then sprinkle with half the garlic, and season with salt and pepper.
2) Grill first on one side then turn them, drizzle with oil once again, and grill on the second side, until the vegetables are lightly browned in spots and firm-tender.
3) Remove from the heat, dice or cut into bite-sized pieces, and toss with the ripe tomatoes and the pesto. Eat warm or cool. If leaving to cool, add the pesto just before serving.

Spinaci (o Verdure) con Mozzarella

A delicious - and easy - way to enjoy fresh spinach. Sometimes I add a light sprinkling of chopped garlic to this, or fresh chives.

SERVES 4

1 bunch	fresh spinach, chard (silver beet) or other similar tender, flavourful greens
1 or 2 balls	fresh mozzarella, as desired
2–3 tbsp	extra virgin olive oil
juice of ¼–½	lemon
	salt and coarsely ground pepper to taste

1) Blanch the greens for just a moment or until they are bright green and just wilted-tender. Remove from the heat and rinse with cold water then gently squeeze dry. Cut into bite-sized pieces and arrange in the centre of a plate.

2) Slice the mozzarella into bite-sized slabs and arrange around the spinach. Drizzle both greens and cheese with olive oil and lemon, and sprinkle with salt and pepper. Enjoy with crusty bread as an *antipasto*.

Chickpeas with Tomatoes

Ceci al' pomadoro is lusty south of Italy fare. Eat it as an *antipasto* or a side dish, or thin it with more tomatoes to make a pasta sauce. Thinned with stock it becomes soup. Leftovers are excellent stirred into risotto.

SERVES 4

1	medium-sized onion, chopped
6 cloves	garlic, coarsely chopped
2–3 tbsp	extra virgin olive oil
1 kg/2¼ lb/6 cups	tomatoes, diced
	or 1½ tins (400 g/14 oz/2⅓ cups each)
	diced tomatoes
1	bay leaf
2 tins (400 g/14 oz/ 2½ cups each)	chickpeas
large pinch of	oregano or thyme leaves, crumbled
pinch of	sugar
	salt and freshly ground black pepper to taste

1) Lightly sauté the onion and garlic in the olive oil until the onion is softened. Add the tomatoes and bay leaf, and cook over a medium-high heat, stirring every so often, until the mixture is sauce-like (5–10 minutes if using tinned tomatoes, about 15 minutes if using fresh).

2) Add the chickpeas, oregano, sugar, salt and pepper, and simmer together until the chickpeas are heated through and permeated with the flavours of the sauce (another 5–10 minutes).

3) Serve either warm or leave to cool and enjoy as a salady *antipasto*.

Melanzane Marinata

Garlicky aubergine (eggplant) slices with roasted peppers in vinaigrette makes a lovely *antipasto*, easily tossed together and able to sit in the refrigerator for up to a week. Just pull it out and place some on a plate while you make the pasta or risotto for the evening meal.

SERVES 4

1	medium-large aubergine (eggplant), sliced crosswise into ½-inch pieces
60 ml/2 fl oz/¼ cup	extra virgin olive oil, or as desired
1–2	roasted red peppers
	or
	several large tbsp full of roasted red pepper strips from a jar
4–6 cloves	garlic, chopped
3–4 tbsp	white wine vinegar, or as desired
	salt and freshly ground black pepper to taste
2–3 tbsp	chopped parsley

1) Arrange the aubergine (eggplant) slices on a baking sheet and brush each side with olive oil. Grill on each side until lightly browned in spots, then layer with the peppers and garlic.
2) Pour the remaining olive oil and vinegar over the cooked aubergine (eggplant), then season with salt and pepper and sprinkle with or toss with parsley.
3) Serve cool, or chill until ready to serve.

Yellow Peppers alla Napoletana

I might follow this slightly sweet-sour-spicy melange of garlicky peppers, tomatoes, capers and olives with Pasta con le Fave (*see Chapter 4, page 65*).

SERVES 4

4 tbsp	extra virgin olive oil
4 cloves	garlic, thinly sliced
4	big yellow peppers, seeded and quartered
2	red peppers, seeded and quartered
2	ripe tomatoes, diced
1 tbsp	tomato purée
1 tsp	sugar, or to taste
1 tbsp	vinegar, or to taste
	salt and freshly ground black pepper to taste
several large pinches of	dried oregano leaves, crumbled
1 tbsp	capers, rinsed if desired
1 tbsp	chopped parsley, preferably flat-leaf

1) Heat the olive oil with the garlic for just a moment, then add the yellow and red peppers and sauté for a few minutes, turning to cook evenly.

2) Add the tomatoes and tomato purée, cook for about 5 minutes, then add the sugar and vinegar, salt, pepper and oregano, and cook over a medium-low heat, covered, stirring every so often, until the peppers are quite tender (about 20 minutes). Stir in the capers and taste for seasoning, then sprinkle with parsley.

3) Leave to cool for a few minutes before serving, or serve cool.

Aubergine (Eggplant) Rolls
Stuffed with Cheese

This Sicilian treat is a typical peasant dish, eaten with crusty country bread, perhaps cooked over an outdoor fire as a snack during the *vendemmia*, when the grapes are being harvested for wine.

Aged caciocavallo cheese is traditionally used for this dish; mozzarella tastes lovely but drips out as it heats up. I prefer halloumi, which though geographically incorrect, works deliciously.

SERVES 4

1	medium sized aubergine (eggplant), cut lengthwise into ¼-inch slices
350 g/12 oz/2 cups	halloumi cheese, cut into slices about ¼-inch thick and about half the length of the aubergine (eggplant) slices
4–6 cloves	garlic, chopped
4–6 tbsp	olive oil, or more as needed
1 tsp	crumbled oregano leaves
1 tbsp	red wine vinegar, or to taste
	salt and pepper
wedges of	lemon
1 tbsp	chopped parsley

1) Arrange the aubergine (eggplant) and the cheese slices on a plate or in a shallow dish. Sprinkle with the garlic, olive oil, oregano and the vinegar, salt and pepper as desired (Halloumi is salty). Leave to sit for about 10 minutes, then take each piece of aubergine (eggplant) and wrap it around a slice of cheese. Seal each bundle with a toothpick.

2) Cook the aubergine (eggplant) parcels either in a ridged grill pan on top of the stove, under a hot grill, or on a barbecue (gas barbecues are excellent for 30-minute Italian cooks), for 4–6 minutes on each side or long enough to brown the aubergine (eggplant) lightly in places and heat the cheese through. Eat right away.

Insalate
Salads

Italian salads – a handful of whatever is leafy and fresh, a scattering of onions, a splash or two of olive oil and a few tangy drips of vinegar, salt, freshly ground black pepper and whatever herb is in the garden – this is a salad. I remember ending a meal in Rome with such a salad and a chunk of rich, pungent local cheese.

In a country like Italy, where the weather can be very sultry indeed for much of the summer, crisp fresh salads are very reviving. And they are fantastic for those with more taste than time and energy.

Bitter Greens, Beetroot and Gorgonzola

Olive oil brings out the best flavours of rich beetroot, bitter greens and the salty, tangy blue cheese.

Rice with Cabbage and Tomatoes (*see page 119*) might follow this very well, or perhaps a pizza with grilled vegetables.

SERVES 4

100-g/3½-oz	pack mixed continental greens, preferably an Italian mixture with chicory
1	shallot, chopped
350 g/12 oz/2 cups or so	cooked beetroot, diced or cubed
175 g/6 oz/1 cup or so	strong, pungent Gorgonzola cheese, in small pieces
3 tbsp	extra virgin olive oil
2 tsp	each red wine vinegar and balsamic vinegar, or use 1 tbsp red wine vinegar only
	freshly ground black pepper to taste

1) Combine the greens with the shallot and arrange the beetroot and cheese over the top. Drizzle with olive oil and vinegars and serve right away, with the pepper grinder for those who desire it.

Orange, Fennel and Green Olive Salad

For an even more refreshing version of this Sicilian salad, add a thinly sliced, peeled and seeded lemon to the dish instead of squeezing it over. Meyer lemons are similar to the sweet-tasting lemons you find in Italy's south.

SERVES 4

3–4	ripe, flavourful oranges, peeled and seeded, and preferably chilled
1–2 cloves	garlic, chopped
1 bulb	fennel, thinly sliced (include some of the wispy green leaves)
3 tbsp	extra virgin olive oil
juice of ½	lemon, or as desired
12–16	cracked green olives

1) Cut the oranges into 6-mm (¼-in) slices. Arrange on a plate and sprinkle with the garlic, then scatter them with the fennel. Dress with olive oil and lemon and garnish with olives.

Smoked Mozzarella (or Tofu) with Tomatoes, Olive Oil and Fresh Basil

The smoky, bland, creamy character of smoked mozzarella or tofu sets off the rich, grassy olive oil, with the fresh, sweet basil putting it all in balance. The smoked mozzarella in this salad gives the flavour of New York's Little Italy, or Italy's sun-drenched south. Smoked tofu is tasty, too; and eating tofu always makes me feel like I'm doing myself a dietary favour.

Serve with crusty bread for dipping.

SERVES 4

250–350 g/8–12 oz/ 1⅓–2 cups	smoked mozzarella or smoked tofu, sliced
2	large, ripe, flavourful tomatoes or 4–5 medium-sized ones or 6–8 small ones, sliced
3 tbsp	extra virgin olive oil, or as desired
1 tsp	balsamic vinegar, or to taste
3 tbsp	fresh basil, thinly sliced or a handful of basil leaves, torn coarsely
12–16	black Niçoise or other small, flavourful black olives

1) Arrange the mozzarella or tofu with the tomatoes on a plate then drizzle generously with olive oil and a sprinkling of the balsamic vinegar. Garnish with the basil and olives.

Salad of Pears, Fennel,
Pecorino Cheese and Walnuts

If lavender-hued chive flowers are available, toss a few into the salad, or a handful of their petals over the top. A mature pecorino cheese is lovely here – it has the nutty, salty tang of Parmesan but the enticing scent of the barnyard, too.

Follow this with a pasta dish, such as Spaghetti with Peas and Lusty Tomato Sauce (*see Chapter 4, page 94*).

SERVES 4

1	small red radicchio, thinly sliced
handful of	arugula (rocket) or other tasty green leaves
1	Belgian endive (chicory), sliced crosswise
1 bulb	fennel, cut into matchsticks or thin slices
2	ripe pears, cut into matchsticks or thin slices
	extra virgin olive oil, to taste
	balsamic or raspberry vinegar, to taste
170–200g/6–8 oz/1–1¼ cups	mature pecorino cheese, thinly sliced or shaved
several tbsp	walnut pieces, either whole or halves

1) Combine the radicchio, arugula (rocket), endive, fennel and pears and arrange on plates. Dress with olive oil and balsamic or raspberry vinegar, then top with a scattering of the cheese and walnuts.

Insalata alla Legumi e Mozzarella

Crunchy chopped vegetables and delicate fresh mozzarella are invigorating, especially combined with crisp salad leaves. Italian salad mixes are much like the French *mesclum*, but often contain more bitter greens such as any of the radicchios. Any mixed continental salad leaves are fine here; if the mixture is not bitter enough, add a handful of sliced raddicchio or frisée lettuce.

SERVES 4

1 yellow and 1 red	pepper, seeded and diced
1	carrot, diced
2	spring onions, thinly sliced
3	tomatoes, diced
3 cloves	of garlic, chopped
2 stalks	of celery, coarsely chopped
3–4 tbsp	olive oil, or as desired
1 tbsp	white wine vinegar, or as desired
1 tsp	balsamic vinegar (optional)
	salt and freshly ground black pepper
several handfuls	of mixed greens
2 tbsp	chopped parsley or any other herb of choice
2	fresh mozzarella cheeses (about 100 g/3½ oz), sliced thickly

1) Combine the yellow and red pepper, carrot, spring onion, tomatoes, garlic and celery and dress with olive oil and the vinegars. Season with salt and pepper.
2) Mix the greens with the parsley or other herbs, then arrange on a plate. Top with mozzarella, then spoon over the mixed vegetables in a pleasing fashion, drizzling a bit of the dressing onto the salad leaves.
3) Serve at once.

Insalata di Patate

Potato salad, Italian style: creamy-fleshed potatoes, dressed in olive oil with spring onions, capers and herbs. Small potatoes cook more quickly than large ones. If your potatoes are large, cut them into halves or quarters. Try to use the plump capers from the island of Pantelleria, which are preserved in salt rather than in vinegar. Rinse and dry them before using; their flavour is a revelation if you've only eaten capers packed in vinegar brine.

This makes a superb summer supper accompanied by ripe, sweet tomatoes, fresh mozzarella and basil, and a little plate of mixed greens that includes puslane if you can find it.

SERVES 4

1 kg/2¼ lb	new potatoes
	salt as desired
3 cloves	garlic, chopped
2–3 tbsp	dry white wine
125 ml/2 fl oz/¼ cup	extra virgin olive oil
3–5	spring onions, including their greens, thinly sliced
3 tbsp	capers
	oregano or marjoram, fresh if possible, to taste
2–3 tbsp	lemon juice or mild wine vinegar to taste
	freshly ground black pepper to taste

1) Boil the potatoes in their skins until they are just tender (about 20 minutes). Drain well and leave in the hot pan on the still-hot stove for a few moments to dry out.
2) Remove their skins, and cut the potatoes into chunks. Add the remaining ingredients and toss gently – I use my hands to keep the potatoes from breaking up and turning to mush.
3) Serve slightly warm or chill until ready to serve.

Variation: Artichoke Heart and Potato Salad

Serve the potato salad tossed with a jar of marinated artichoke hearts.

Arugula with Mango or Peach and Shaved Parmesan

If I'm serving this as an *antipasto* or little nibble I use 40 g/1½ oz/½ cup rocket; if serving it as a salad, I use double or even triple the amount for its distinctive tangy, peppery flavour.

I might follow this with polenta layered with tomatoes, cheese and fresh rosemary, or Spaghetti alla Norma (*see Chapter 4, page 101*).

SERVES 4

40 g/1½ oz/½ cup	arugula (rocket)
1	ripe mango, peeled and cut into bite-sized pieces or 2 ripe peaches or nectarines, cut into bite-sized pieces
60–90 g/2–3 oz/1–1½ cups	Parmesan cheese, thinly shaved
	olive oil, as desired, for drizzling
	balsamic vinegar, to taste

1) Arrange the arugula (rocket) on a plate, then place the mango and cheese over it. Dress with olive oil and balsamic vinegar to taste. Serve right away.

Cherry Tomatoes with Goat's Cheese and Basil

Serve with good bread to scoop into the tomatoes, herbs and cheese. Leave the tomatoes whole, or cut them into halves for easier eating. A traditional cheese would be a goat's cheese from Sicily or a fresh pecorino from Sardinia, but feta is easily available, and its salty, fresh and sparkling flavour is perfect with the basil, olive oil and tomatoes.

Follow with Pappardelle with Sage and Black Olives (*see Chapter 4, page 85*).

SERVES 4

600 g/1½ lb	cherry tomatoes, halved
175–250 g/6–8 oz/1⅓ cups	feta cheese (or fresh pecorino), cut into bite-sized pieces or diced
30 g/1 oz/1 cup	or several handfuls basil leaves, torn
½	a red or mild white onion, chopped
1 clove	garlic, chopped
3–4 tbsp	olive oil, or as desired
1–2 tbsp	red wine vinegar

1) Combine all the ingredients and eat right away or chill until ready to eat.

Tomato and Sweetcorn Salad with Basil

This insalata di pomodori comes from a beach picnic on a Sardinian shore – sweetcorn is not what I associate with Italian food, but it is delicious in this salad. And what is polenta, anyway? Corn!

Serve before a plate of Pasta with Courgettes (Zucchini) (*see Chapter 4, page 82*).

SERVES 4

4 ears of	sweetcorn
8	ripe, sweet, juicy tomatoes, sliced
¼	red onion, thinly sliced
1 clove	garlic, chopped
pinch each of	sugar and salt
1 tbsp	red wine vinegar
3 tbsp	extra virgin olive oil
60 g/2 oz/1 cup	Parmesan cheese, thinly shaved
(approximately)	
4–6 tbsp	thinly sliced fresh basil

1) Cook the sweetcorn until just tender. This will depend on the sweetcorn itself: the younger it is the less time it takes to cook; generally, a few minutes is all you need. Remove from the heat and leave to cool until you can handle it (5 minutes or so).
2) Cut the kernels off the cobs and set aside.
3) Arrange the tomatoes on a plate and sprinkle with the red onion, garlic, sugar, salt, vinegar and olive oil. Top with a scattering of Parmesan and basil. Serve right away.

Sautéed Mushrooms with Salad Leaves

Exotic, or wild-ish, mushrooms (funghi) are increasingly available, even in our local delis and supermarkets. When it is mushroom season in Italy, the forests are alive with foragers, all out to stalk the wild porcini or the little ovoli or even a truffle or two.

This salad is a quickly sautéed little number of mushrooms served on a bed of greens – the greens wilt, effectively making a warm salad. A handful of toasted pinenuts makes a good crisp counterpoint – and if you don't have the time to toast them, they're good raw as well.

If you don't wish to serve this on a bed of salady greens, eat it as a topping for a creamy pasta, or stir it into a risotto, or spoon over garlicky toast. It's good, too, as a side dish. Shaved Parmesan makes a delicious addition to this recipe – scatter it over the warm mushrooms and wilting greens as abundantly and generously as you desire.

SERVES 4

500 g/1 lb/4½ cups	mixed fresh mushrooms: chanterelles, porcini, oyster etc.
5 tbsp	olive oil or combination of olive oil and butter, or as desired
3 cloves	garlic, finely chopped
	salt to taste and a tiny pinch of cayenne pepper (as black pepper can be a little funny with certain mushrooms)
80–125 g/3–4 oz/1⅓ cups	mixed salad greens, preferably Italian style, with arugula (rocket), frisée, chicory, raddichio, etc.

juice of 1 lemon

bunch of chives, finely chopped

1) Wipe the mushrooms with a damp cloth and trim off any tough or dry bits; slice the mushrooms into bite-sized pieces.

2) Sauté the mushrooms in the olive oil or olive oil and butter combined, reserving a tbsp or two of the olive oil to toss with the greens. When the mushrooms are almost lightly browned and tender (about 3 minutes), stir in the garlic, season with salt (and cayenne if using) and remove from the heat.

3) Toss the greens with the reserved olive oil and the juice of ½ the lemon, then spoon the mushrooms over it. Squirt the lemon over the salad, sprinkle with the chives, and serve right away.

Countryside Salad with Garlic Croutons

For an informal supper meal, serve a chunk of creamy rustic cheese – Italian preferably – alongside the salad, as I enjoyed one sweltering evening in Rome not long ago.

SERVES 4

90 g/3 oz/1 cup	radicchio
90 g/3 oz/1 cup	baby lettuce salad mixture
60 g/2 oz/²/₃ cup	rocket leaves (arugula)
60 g/2 oz/²/₃ cup	frisée or curly chicory
1	shallot or other small, flavourful onion, chopped
6 tbsp	extra virgin olive oil
	salt and coarsely ground black pepper
125–175 g/4–6 oz (approximately)	country bread, preferably a day or two old, cut into cubes
2 cloves	garlic, chopped
2–3 tsp	red wine vinegar, or to taste

1) Cut the radicchio, baby lettuces, rocket leaves and frisee all into bite-sized pieces then mix with the shallot or onion. Toss with several tbsp of the olive oil, and add salt and pepper to taste.

2) Heat the remaining olive oil in a frying pan and brown the bread cubes until they are golden and crunchy. Remove from the heat and toss with the garlic.

3) Toss the salad with the vinegar, then with the hot, garlicky croutons and serve.

Minestre
Soups

Italian soups are hearty, delicious, and wholesome. But if you think that they take a long time to simmer and cook, you are happily mistaken. There are many, many soups with Italian vegetables, aromatics and herbs, as well as pastas and beans, that take mere minutes to prepare. Following is a handful of my current favourites.

Broad (Fava) Bean Soup with Tiny Pastas

If your broad beans are anything but young, you should probably take the time to peel them – a secret to their success is to
blanch them, and when they are warm but cool enough to handle, just tear open the skin with your fingernails and push them
out. I have not added the shelling time needed for the broad
beans – you might be very quick; indeed, you might use frozen
broad beans. But then if you are a neophyte, it could take a lot
longer than you anticipate.

SERVES 4

200–300g/8–12 oz/	broad beans (favas)
or	
90–125 g/3–4 oz/1–1½ cups	½ cup shelled (frozen is fine)
125 g/6 oz	small pastas of choice – either very small shells, macaroni, etc. or tiny pastina such as stelline, alphabets or orzo
1	small onion, chopped
3 cloves	garlic, chopped
3 tbsp	extra virgin olive oil
2 tbsp	chopped parsley
1 litre/1¾ pints/5 cups	vegetable stock (water mixed with a stock cube is fine)
	salt and freshly ground black pepper
	freshly grated Parmesan cheese, as desired

1) Shell the beans and blanch them, then peel if they are not young and supple.
2) Meanwhile, cook the pasta until *al dente*, then drain.
3) Sauté the onion with half the garlic in the olive oil until the onion is softened, then sprinkle in the parsley and peeled beans and cook for a few moments together.
4) Add the stock, bring to the boil, then simmer for 5 minutes or until the beans are tender and the soup is flavourful. Add the remaining garlic and the pasta, heat it through, and season with salt and pepper.
5) Serve right away, with Parmesan or pecorino on the side to be spooned in as desired.

Minestra alla Giardino

The name means soup from the garden, and it does indeed welcome a variety of vegetables. Whichever vegetables are in season will probably go happily into the pot; allow for cooking times, and enjoy whatever is the freshest of the moment. Not only are vegetables in season the tastiest and healthiest, they are cheapest as well. And very Italian.

SERVES 4

1 litre/1¾ pints/5 cups	vegetable stock
5 cloves	garlic, sliced
1	small carrot, diced
1 stalk	celery, chopped
3	medium-sized ripe tomatoes, diced
175–250 g/6–8 oz	green beans, topped and tailed and cut into small pieces
1	yellow courgette (zucchini), if available, otherwise 1 green courgette (zucchini)
175 g/6 oz	small pasta for soup
1 clove	garlic, chopped
1 tsp	chopped fresh rosemary
2–3 tbsp	extra virgin olive oil
	salt and freshly ground black pepper

1) Combine the stock with the sliced garlic, the carrot, celery and tomatoes. Bring to the boil and cook for about 10 minutes or until the mixture is fragrant and the vegetables are nearly tender.

2) Meanwhile, cook the pasta. Drain and set aside.

3) Add to the soup the green beans and yellow courgette (zucchini) and cook for about 5 minutes or until the vegetables are just tender.

4) Stir in the garlic, rosemary and olive oil, then the pasta. Season with salt and pepper and serve right away. (If the pasta is quite cold, it will need to be reheated for a few minutes in the hot soup.)

Tomato Broth with Peas and Little Pastas

Peas and small round macaroni float in this tomatoey soup. Sometimes I make this with tiny pastina and fresh fennel instead of ditalini and peas, or pastina and asparagus (omitting the fennel seeds if using asparagus), with variations that are nearly endless depending on the market and garden. Whichever you choose, it takes only a few minutes to rustle up.

This is a nice soup to precede a plate of Pan-grilled Mediterranean Vegetables (*see Chapter 6, page 136*), or perhaps Melanzane con Ricotta (*see Chapter 6, page 140*).

SERVES 4

½	small onion, chopped
3 cloves	garlic, chopped
1 tbsp	extra virgin olive oil
6–8	ripe tomatoes, diced (tinned are okay, but fresh are preferable)
pinch each of	fennel seeds and mixed Italian herbs or marjoram
1 litre/1¾ pints/5 cups	vegetable stock (or water mixed with 1–2 stock cubes)
175 g/6 oz	ditalini or other small pasta shapes
115 g/4 oz/1 cup	peas, either fresh and blanched or frozen
	salt and freshly ground black pepper to taste
	freshly grated Parmesan, as desired

1) Lightly sauté the onion and garlic in the olive oil until softened, then stir in the tomatoes, fennel seeds, herbs and stock. Bring to the boil, then lower the heat and simmer for about 5 minutes.
2) Meanwhile, cook the pasta until *al dente*. Drain.
3) Add the peas to the soup and heat through. Add the drained pasta, and season with salt and pepper. Serve sprinkled generously with Parmesan.

Tortelloni Soup with Green Vegetables

Almost all stuffed pasta is delicious served in a vegetable-rich stock – you could make this soup every night for months and it would be different, depending on what sort of filling and pasta, what shape and size of tortelloni, tortellini, ravioli, etc. you used. Similarly for the vegetables – it is a soup that follows the seasons.

The last-minute enrichment of olive oil mixed with herbs gives a fragrant lift. You might enjoy whipping together a frittata and simple salad of baby lettuces and herbs to go with this soup for a summery supper.

SERVES 4–6

350 g/12 oz	tortelloni of choice, especially ones with green pasta
1 litre/1¾ pints/5 cups	vegetable stock or water mixed with 2 stock cubes
2	courgettes (zucchini), diced or 1 bunch broccoli, diced or a handful of green beans, diced, spinach or chard leaves or any combination of green vegetables, diced
2–3 tbsp	extra virgin olive oil
2 tbsp	chopped chives or 1 spring onion, finely chopped
1 tbsp	chopped fresh mixed herbs such as marjoram, sage, oregano, etc.

1) Cook the tortelloni until *al dente*. Drain.
2) Combine the stock with the vegetables and bring to the boil; cook until the vegetables are just bright green and *al dente*.
3) Mix the olive oil with the chives or spring onion and the herbs.
4) Spoon the hot pastas into 4 bowls and ladle the hot vegetable soup over it. Serve each with a spoonful of the herb oil on top.

Courgette (zucchini) Soup with Herbs

A little dry white wine lifts this dish and adds a certain refined tang and finesse to what is otherwise a simple soup.

SERVES 4

1 litre/1¾ pints/5 cups	vegetable stock (or water mixed with 1 or 2 stock cubes)
125 ml/4 fl oz/½ cup	dry white wine
1 tsp	each fresh rosemary leaves and fresh marjoram, finely chopped
450 g/1 lb/4 cups	young courgettes (zucchini), cut into bite-sized chunks
	Salt and black or cayenne (red) pepper to taste
90 g/3 oz	pastina of choice, such as stelline or orzo
3 cloves	garlic, chopped
2 tbsp	olive oil
2–3 tbsp	fresh basil, thinly shredded
	freshly grated Parmesan or pecorino, to taste

1) Combine the stock with the wine, rosemary, marjoram, and courgettes (zucchini) in a saucepan and bring to the boil. Reduce the heat and simmer until the courgettes (zucchini) are very tender (15 to 20 minutes). Season with salt and black or red pepper.
2) Meanwhile, cook the pasta until *al dente*. Drain.
3) Heat the garlic in the olive oil until it is fragrant and slightly golden. Set it aside.
4) When the courgettes (zucchini) are tender, add the sautéed garlic to the soup along with the pasta. Heat through and serve, sprinkled generously with the basil and cheese.

Broccoli Soup

This easy soup consists of little more than bright, jade-green broccoli floating in garlicky broth. The herbs and Parmesan add their distinctive character.

Since the soup is so light, a casserole of Mazzamurru *(see Chapter 6, page 156)* would make a hearty autumn meal.

1 bunch	broccoli, cut into small bite-sized pieces
3 cloves	garlic, coarsely chopped
1 litre/1¾ pints/5 cups	vegetable stock (or water mixed with 2 vegetable stock cubes)
2–3 tbsp	chopped herbs: parsley, marjoram, basil, etc.
3–4 tbsp	freshly grated Parmesan cheese, or to taste

1) Combine the broccoli with the garlic and the stock in a saucepan and bring to the boil. Reduce the heat and simmer for 5–10 minutes or until the broccoli is bright green.

2) Remove from the heat and stir in the herbs. Serve each bowl-ful steaming hot, sprinkled generously with Parmesan.

Pappa al Pomodoro

Pappa is legendary: tomato soup, thickened with bread, and eaten with lots of olive oil drizzled onto it at the table. It is lusty, unrefined, and you may balk at the first spoonful. But each mouthful of this soothing soup tastes better and better. It is the sort of soup that one craves, every so often.

SERVES 4

1	onion, chopped
5 cloves	garlic, thinly sliced
3 tbsp	olive oil, plus extra for drizzling
350–400 g/12–14 oz/2–2⅓ cups	diced tomatoes (tinned is okay, include the juices)
1 litre/1¾ pints/5 cups	vegetable stock, or water mixed with 1–2 stock cubes, to taste
6–8	thick slices country-style bread, especially sourdough bread, cut into small pieces
2 cloves	garlic, crushed with a pinch of salt
	sprinkling of cayenne pepper
	capers (rinse well of their vinegar brine, then dry, or use salt-dried capers), to taste, or salt to taste
	chopped parsley, rocket, oregano, or basil, to taste

1) Lightly sauté the onion with the sliced garlic in the olive oil until softened, then add the tomatoes and cook for a few moments together.

2) Add the stock, bring to the boil, then lower the heat and simmer together 5 minutes. Add about ½ of the bread, simmer together until the bread is mushy (about 5 minutes), then whirl the soup in a the blender to purée it.

3) Add the crushed garlic, and serve with the rest of the bread floating in it like croutons, and with a generous drizzling of olive oil in each bowl. Sprinkle with cayenne, capers, and whichever fresh herb you choose: parsley, basil, oregano or rocket.

Minestrone al Pesto

While most minestrones are at their best when long simmered and reheated, this is a quickly prepared, fresh little soup that needs only a spoonful of pesto to enliven it.

Green beans, peas or yellow squash are all vegetables that could go into a summer minestrone such as this one. And if you have no cannellini beans, use borlotti, or even butter beans.

1	leek, diced
1	carrot, thinly sliced or diced
1	stalk celery, diced
3–5 cloves	garlic, coarsely chopped
2 tbsp	extra virgin olive oil
2	small waxy potatoes, peeled and cut into chunks
400 g/14 oz/2⅓ cups	diced tomatoes (tinned is fine, include their juices)
1 litre/1¾ pints/5 cups	vegetable stock (or water mixed with 1–2 stock cubes)
several leaves	spinach or chard, thinly sliced
¼ head	cabbage, thinly sliced or cut into bite-sized chunks
2	courgettes (zucchini), diced or sliced
Sprig	fresh rosemary, marjoram or oregano (optional)
400 g/14 oz/2 cups	cooked drained white beans such as cannellini
	salt and freshly ground black pepper to taste
3–5 tbsp	pesto, or as desired
	Parmesan cheese, as desired, freshly grated

1) Combine the leek, carrot, celery and garlic, olive oil, potatoes, tomatoes and stock in a soup pot. Bring to the boil, cook over a high heat for about 10 minutes or until the vegetables are about half tender, then add the spinach or chard, the cabbage, the courgettes (zucchini) and the rosemary. Continue to cook for another 10 minutes or until the cabbage is tender.

2) Add the beans and heat through, taste for seasoning, adding salt and pepper as necessary, and serve right away, each bowl garnished with a spoonful of pesto and a sprinkling of Parmesan.

Chickpea and Potato Soup-Stew

For a quicker dish, cut the potatoes into small pieces. You can serve this with cooked pasta added, or with garlic croutons or toasts to dunk in. Sometimes I like a hit of hot pepper, too.

SERVES 4

2	small to medium onions, chopped
5 cloves	garlic, chopped
2–3 tbsp	extra virgin olive oil
3	waxy potatoes (about 450g/1 lb/3 cups in total), peeled and cut into bite-sized chunks
400 g/14 oz/2⅓ cups	diced tomatoes (tinned are fine, include the juices; if using fresh, add a tbsp of tomato purée to the mixture)
2–3 tbsp	fresh rosemary, chopped
1 litre/1¾ pints/5 cups	vegetable stock (or water mixed with a vegetable stock cube)
400 g/14 oz/2⅓ cups	cooked, drained chickpeas (tinned is fine)
	salt and coarsely ground black pepper, to taste
1 tbsp	chopped parsley
	freshly grated Parmesan, as desired
	more extra virgin olive oil, for drizzling (optional)

1) Lightly sauté the onion and garlic in the olive oil until softened, then add the potatoes and cook for a few moments. Add the tomatoes, rosemary and stock and bring to the boil. Cook over medium-high heat until the tomatoes are almost tender (about 15 minutes), then add the chickpeas and warm through. Taste for seasoning.
2) Serve sprinkled with parsley and Parmesan, and offer more olive oil as desired.

Tuscan Bean Soup with Chard

Hefty high-fibre minestra di fagioli is a snap to toss together using tinned beans, well-rinsed to rid them of their salty brine from the can.

If desired, spoon *al dente* macaroni or pasta shapes into the hot soup before serving, or serve the soup ladled over thick slices of toasted stale bread.

SERVES 4

1	medium to large potato, peeled and diced
5	ripe tomatoes, diced
3 cloves	garlic, sliced
1 litre/1¾ pints/5 cups	vegetable stock (or water mixed with 1–2 vegetable stock cubes)
1 tin (400 g/14 oz/2 cups)	borlotti beans, drained and rinsed in cold water
1 tin (400 g/14 oz/2 cups)	cannellini beans, drained and rinsed in cold water
several large pinches each of	rosemary, sage and basil
1–2 tbsp	extra virgin olive oil, plus more to serve
½ bunch	chard leaves (silver beet), thinly sliced
	freshly grated Parmesan cheese, as desired

1) Combine the potato with half the tomatoes, the garlic and the vegetable stock and bring to the boil. Cook over a high heat until the potato is tender (about 5–8 minutes).

2) Whirl the potato and tomato in the blender with the borlotti beans until smooth then return to the pot and add the rest of the tomatoes, the cannellini beans, the rosemary, sage and basil, and a tbsp of the olive oil.

3) Bring to the boil again, then lower the heat slightly and cook over a medium heat until the tomatoes fall apart into the sauce. Lightly mash some of the cannellini beans with a masher, leaving most of them whole, and add the chard leaves, cooking for a few more minutes or until the chard is bright green and tender.

4) Serve hot, ladled into bowls sprinkled generously with Parmesan and drizzled with olive oil.

Zuppa di Fagioli e Funghi

Earthy beans and equally earthy – though ultra-luxurious – wild mushrooms is one of the treats of a Tuscan autumn. I love this rustic soup with a few little plates of *antipasti* on the side: things like cooked spinach, roasted peppers or roasted fennel.

SERVES 4

2 tins (400 g/14 oz/2 cups)	borlotti beans, or 750 g/1½ lb/3½ cups cooked borlotti beans
a few sprigs	of fresh rosemary or savory
15–30 g/½–1 oz	dried mushrooms such as porcini, trompettes de mort etc., broken into small pieces
1 litre/1¾ pints/5 cups	of vegetable stock (or water mixed with 1–2 vegetable stock cubes)
1	onion, chopped
5 cloves	garlic, chopped
4 tbsp	olive oil
2	ripe tomatoes, grated (fresh is best; tinned, chopped tomatoes are acceptable, just)
	salt and freshly ground black pepper to taste
optional to serve:	thick slices of country bread lightly toasted in the oven, and extra virgin olive oil for drizzling in each bowlful

1) Combine the beans with the rosemary or savory, the mushrooms and the stock and bring to the boil.

2) Meanwhile, sauté the onion and garlic in the olive oil. When softened, add the tomatoes and cook down until it is a saucey, oniony mixture. Add this to the simmering bean and mushroom soup and cook over medium heat for 15–20 minutes or until the flavour is rich and appealing.

3) Season with salt and pepper and enjoy ladled over crusty garlic-rubbed toast, with an extra drizzle of olive oil if desired.

Paste
Pastas

The pasta chapter in this book is predictably long. Indeed, few foods typify *cucina* Italiana as does pasta: eaten twice a day in much of Italy, seldom boring for its wealth of shapes and sizes and delicious variety of sauces. And for a vegetarian, especially one without a great deal of time to prepare the meals, pasta is an important food.

It is perhaps the quickest of dishes – the time you need is mostly for preparing sauce – and so many sauces are as quick to throw together as they are satisfying to eat. Pasta is healthy, too, a natural companion for vegetables of the seasons, the earthy richness of legumes and beans, the fragrance of herbs.

You can enjoy pasta as a first course, in the traditional Italian style, or as a main course in a more contemporary way. It's good for lunch, dinner, supper and even midnight feasts.

Hot Pasta with a Cool Sauce

The hot pasta barely warms the salady, garlicky tomato sauce. Delicious and refreshing fare when the weather is sultry and your kitchen too hot to cook in. Oh, and tomatoes are deliciously ripe.

SERVES 4

8–10	ripe tomatoes, diced
1 tbsp	balsamic or red wine vinegar
pinch	of sugar, to balance the acidity of the tomatoes
	salt to taste
3 cloves	of garlic, chopped
handful	of fresh basil leaves, coarsely chopped or torn
375 g/12 oz	elbow pasta or long pasta such as spaghetti
3 tbsp	extra virgin olive oil
125 g/4 oz/²/₃ cup	fresh mozzarella, diced

1) Combine the tomatoes with the vinegar, sugar, salt, garlic and basil and leave to stand while you cook the pasta.
2) Cook the pasta until *al dente*, then drain, mix with the olive oil and tomato mixture, then toss in the mozzarella. Serve right away.

Stock-Cooked Orzo with Lemon and Parsley

I first tasted this in Venice where it was cooked in the stock made from boiling fish, and dressed with crunchy fried breadcrumbs. I prefer it in vegetable stock for its lightness and vivacity. Any type of pasta is interesting cooked in stock – but take care to dress it simply afterwards. Olive oil and lemon show off its simplicity, as does the freshness of a sprinkling of parsley.

SERVES 4

1 litre/1¾ pints/5 cups	vegetable stock (or water mixed with 1–2 vegetable stock cubes)
375 g/12 oz	orzo or other small pasta
1–2 tbsp	extra virgin olive oil
1–2 cloves	garlic, chopped
juice of 1–2	lemons, or to taste
30 g/1 oz/½ cup	parsley, chopped
	salt and freshly ground black pepper, to taste

1) Bring the stock to the boil, add the pasta and cook until *al dente*. Drain the pasta and reserve the stock for later use.
2) Toss the orzo with the olive oil and garlic, then with the lemon juice, parsley, salt and pepper. Serve right away.

Tender Pasta with Pesto and Goat's Cheese

In Liguria, the pasta is prepared from a delicate dough made with white wine, and dressed with fragrant pesto made from the basil that is present everywhere, growing in every window box and wafting out into the streets from *trattorie*. Do seek a good quality pesto, preferably one from a good deli, as this can make all the difference in this dish. You can use any fresh pasta available, or even Chinese or Japanese noodles, as long as they are delicate and cut into wide squares or circles.

As this is a light little pasta, I might serve a bowl of Vegetable Stew with Olive Oil and Lemon (*see Chapter 6, page 138*) for a main course.

SERVES 4

12–16 oz	flat, wide, delicate squares or circles of fresh pasta, wonton wrappers or gyoza wrappers. You can use egg roll wrappers, but they need to be cut into a manageable size.
45 g/1½ oz	butter
200 g/7 oz	pesto, or as desired
90 g/3 oz/¾ cup	goat's cheese, crumbled

1) Boil the pasta until just tender, only a minute or two. Drain carefully so as not to break the pasta.
2) Toss the drained pasta with the butter and pesto, then sprinkle with the goat's cheese. Serve right away.

Whole-wheat Pasta with Goat's Cheese, Tomatoes and Olives

Whole-wheat spaghetti can be heavy and doughy, so take care to buy only Italian whole-wheat pasta as it is firm and flavourful.

SERVES 4

375–500 g/12–16 oz	whole-wheat spaghetti
15 black and 15 green	olives, preferably Italian, stoned and coarsely chopped
3 cloves	garlic, chopped
4	ripe tomatoes, diced, or 250 g/8 oz/ 1 cup diced tinned tomatoes
90 ml/3 fl oz/⅓ cup	extra virgin olive oil
125 g/4 oz/1 cup	goat's cheese, coarsely crumbled
several handfuls	of fresh basil, torn or coarsely cut up
	freshly ground black pepper to taste

1) Cook the pasta until *al dente*.
2) Meanwhile, combine the olives with the garlic, tomatoes and olive oil.
3) Drain the pasta and toss with the olive mixture then toss in the goat's cheese, basil and pepper. Serve right away.

Spicy Whole-wheat Spaghetti with Broccoli

Though whole-wheat spaghetti is my favourite for this recipe –
nutty tasting, full of goodness and vitamins – the dish is also
very good prepared with ordinary spaghetti, imported from Italy,
of course!

SERVES 4

375–500 g/12–16 oz	whole-wheat spaghetti
1 large bunch	of broccoli, cut into small florets, the stem peeled and diced
8–10 garlic cloves,	peeled and coarsely chopped or sliced
4–6 tbsp	extra virgin olive oil
1	dried red chilli, broken into several pieces or hot red pepper flakes, to taste
	salt and freshly ground black pepper, to taste

1) Cook the spaghetti until about half-tender, then add the broccoli and continue cooking until the pasta and broccoli are both *al dente*.

2) Meanwhile, heat the garlic in the olive oil with the chilli pepper in a heavy frying pan. When the garlic is just golden, remove it from the heat. Remove the chunks of hot pepper and discard. Set the flavoured oil and garlic aside.

3) Drain the pasta and broccoli and toss with the reserved garlic and olive oil mixture. Season with salt and pepper to taste.

Penne with Sun-dried Tomato and Goat's Cheese Cream

The combination of soft goat's cheese and sparky sun-dried tomatoes mixes into a creamy yet pungent sauce. It is embarrassingly easy and quick to put together, with a flavour suitable for company. Serve with plates of cooked seasonal vegetables – such as coarsely chopped spinach, asparagus, young peas, broad beans, roasted peppers – for each diner to take a few spoonfuls and garnish his or her plate of pasta with.

SERVES 4

375–500 g/12–16 oz	penne, lumache or other chunky pasta
20	sun-dried tomatoes (soft, marinated, either homemade or from a jar), cut into strips
3–4 cloves	garlic, chopped
3 tbsp	olive oil, or to taste
	salt and freshly ground black pepper to taste
½ tsp	dried thyme leaves or 1 tsp fresh marjoram, or to taste
155 g/5 oz/1¼ cups	fresh goat's cheese, coarsely crumbled

1) Cook pasta until *al dente*.
2) Meanwhile, combine the rest of the ingredients. For a smooth creamy sauce, if desired, whirl it in the blender.
3) Drain the pasta, toss with the remaining ingredients and serve right away.

Spaghetti with Double Tomato Salsa and Fresh Mozzarella

Sun-dried tomatoes and fresh, ripe, summery tomatoes combine in this pasta, redolent of basil and garlic and studded with bites of fresh mozzarella.

SERVES 4–6

500 g/1 lb	spaghetti
6–8	very ripe tomatoes, diced
15	sun-dried tomatoes, the soft, marinated kind from a jar, coarsely chopped or thinly sliced into strips
several large handfuls	of fresh basil, thinly sliced or coarsely chopped
3 cloves	garlic, chopped
4 tbsp	extra virgin olive oil
	salt and freshly ground black pepper to taste
2 balls	of fresh mozzarella, diced

1) Cook the spaghetti until *al dente*.
2) Meanwhile, combine the fresh and sun-dried tomatoes with the basil, garlic and olive oil. Taste for seasoning, adding salt, pepper and more garlic if needed.
3) Drain the spaghetti, then toss with the sauce and mozzarella cheese. Serve right away.

Pasta con le Fave

Pasta with broad beans and goat's cheese is a lovely springtime dish. When broad beans are very young you do not need to peel them; as they grow older they are far nicer peeled, though this task takes a while to perform.

A starter or side dish of Grilled Pesto Asparagus *(see Chapter 6, page 148)* would be very nice with this.

SERVES 4

500 g/1 lb	pasta, such as spaghetti
375 g/12 oz/1¾ cups	young broad beans
5 cloves	garlic, chopped
3 tbsp	extra virgin olive oil
125 ml/4 oz/1 cup	goat's cheese, crumbled
	salt and freshly ground black pepper to taste
handful	of basil leaves, coarsely chopped, or 1 tsp fresh marjoram, chopped

1) Cook the pasta until nearly tender then add the broad beans and continue cooking until the beans are just tender and the pasta is *al dente*. Drain.
2) Toss the hot pasta and broad beans with the garlic, olive oil and goat's cheese. Season with salt and pepper then serve garnished with either basil or marjoram.

Macaroni con Pomadori

A tomatoey sauce cloaks the pasta, enriched by the pungent, garlicky seasoning paste added at the last minute. Serve following a
Salad of Pears, Fennel, Pecorino Cheese and Walnuts (*see Chapter 2, page 23*).

SERVES 4

2	onions, thinly sliced
4 tbsp	extra virgin olive oil
8 cloves	of garlic
salt, as needed	
pinch	of sugar (about ⅛–¼ tsp)
1 kg/ 2¼ lb/6 cups	fresh tomatoes or 2 tins (400 g/14 oz/1¾ cups each) tinned tomatoes, diced
¼	fresh hot green chilli, chopped
1 tsp or to taste	hot chilli seasoning such as garlic-chilli paste or a few shakes of bottled hot pepper sauce
450 g/1 lb	macaroni
generous pinch	of oregano
	freshly ground black pepper as desired

1) Lightly sauté the onions in half the olive oil until they have softened. While they are cooking, slice half of the garlic thinly, then add to the pan. When the onions and garlic are both softened and the onion is lightly golden in places, sprinkle with salt and sugar, then stir in the tomatoes. Cook over a high heat for about 10 minutes, or until the sauce is slightly thickened and flavourful. Stir in the chilli, hot pepper sauce and set aside.

2) Crush the garlic with a large pinch of salt, then work in the remaining olive oil to make a paste. Set it aside.

3) Cook the pasta in rapidly boiling salted water until *al dente*, then drain and toss with the pasta sauce, then with the garlic-olive oil paste. Serve heaped onto a platter or into a bowl and sprinkle with oregano and pepper.

Garlicky Pasta with Fresh Green Herbs

The flavour and character of the dish depends on the choice and quantity of the herbs used. Use larger amounts of mild herbs such as parsley, and smaller amounts of pungent herbs such as oregano, rosemary or sage.

I might begin the meal with a tomatoey soup (*see Chapter 3*), and finish with Grilled Peaches with Ripe Blackberries (*see Chapter 8, page 196*).

SERVES 4

500 g/1 lb	spaghetti
8 cloves	garlic, chopped
60–90 ml/2–3 fl oz/¼–⅓ cup	extra virgin olive oil
selection	of chopped, fresh herbs: about 30 g/1 oz in total. Choose from parsley, mint, basil, chives, marjoram, thyme, sage, oregano, rosemary, tarragon, etc.
	salt and freshly ground black pepper to taste

1) Cook the spaghetti until *al dente*.
2) Meanwhile, heat the garlic in the olive oil until it smells fragrant, just a few moments, then toss the herbs into the hot, garlicky oil. Remove from the heat.
3) Drain the pasta and toss it in the pan with the garlicky oil and herbs. Season generously with salt and black pepper and serve right away.

Penne con Asparagi

Sun-dried tomatoes add their savour to this lusty dish of pasta and asparagus. Begin with several *antipasti*, including sizzling Red Pepper Rolls Stuffed with Melted Cheese (*see Chapter 1, page 9*). To accompany the pasta, you could serve a simple salad of mixed leaves including arugula (rocket).

SERVES 4–6

500 g/1 lb	penne
250 g/8 oz	asparagus, tough ends broken off, the stalks cut into bite-sized pieces
2–3 tbsp	olive oil
2–3 cloves	garlic, chopped
2–3	diced, fresh tomatoes plus 1 tbsp tomato purée, or 2–3 tbsp diced tomatoes from a tin
10	sun-dried tomatoes, coarsely chopped
3 tbsp	thinly sliced basil or 1 tbsp pesto
60 g/2 oz/1 cup	Parmesan cheese, shaved

1) Cook the pasta until about half-tender, then add the asparagus and continue to cook until the pasta is *al dente* and the asparagus just cooked through.
2) Meanwhile, combine the olive oil, garlic, tomatoes, sun-dried tomatoes and basil or pesto.
3) Drain the pasta and asparagus, then toss with the tomatoey sauce and serve hot, tossed with about half the cheese and garnished with scatterings of the rest.

Spaghetti with Garlic Butter and Walnuts

Golden sautéed garlic is combined with warm toasted nuts, then tossed with spaghetti, Parmesan cheese and a small amount of cream or mascarpone for this rich Ligurian dish. This sauce can also be puréed, and as such is brilliant with spinach-filled ravioli.

Cooked broccoli at room temperature as a *contorno* (*see Chapter 6, page 149*), and perhaps a plate of roasted peppers as well, makes a tasty supper. Finish with a plate of ripe pears for dessert, with a deliciously pungent cheese such as stracchino, and perhaps a glass of grappa.

SERVES 4

375 g/12 oz	spaghetti
4–6 cloves	garlic, chopped
60 g/2 oz/¼ cup	butter
125 g/4 oz/1 cup	shelled walnuts, coarsely chopped
125 ml/4 fl oz/½ cup	whipping cream or 3–4 tbsp mascarpone
45 g/1½ oz/¾ cup	Parmesan cheese, freshly grated
	salt and freshly ground black pepper, to taste

1) Cook the spaghetti until *al dente*.
2) Meanwhile, sauté the garlic in the butter until fragrant and lightly golden, then add the walnuts and swirl around in the garlicky butter. Remove from the heat and stir in the cream or mascarpone. Set aside.
3) Drain the spaghetti. Toss it with the sauce, then with the cheese and season with salt and pepper to taste. Serve right away.

Farfalle al' Broccoli e Piselli

Hearty and robust, this dish of butterfly shaped pasta with broccoli, peas and tomato-pepper sauce is indestructible, and can be varied at whim. I often serve it with a dollop of snowy ricotta.

SERVES 4

4–6 cloves	garlic, chopped
½–1	red or yellow sweet pepper, diced
3 tbsp	extra virgin olive oil
1 bunch	broccoli, broken into florets, the stem peeled and diced
several heaped tbsp	fresh blanched or frozen small peas
400 g/14 oz/1¾ cups	tinned diced tomatoes (if using fresh, use 500 g/1 lb/3 cups and add 1 tbsp tomato purée)
¼ tsp	cayenne pepper or other hot pepper seasoning
generous pinch	of thyme
375–500 g/12–16 oz	bow tie pasta, preferably green or multi-coloured vegetable pastas
	salt and freshly ground black pepper to taste
	grated Parmesan or pecorino cheese, as desired

1) Lightly sauté the garlic and sweet pepper in the olive oil. Add the broccoli and a few tbsp of water and cook over a high heat for a minute or two until half-tender. Add the peas and tomatoes and cook over a high heat for 5–10 minutes. Season with cayenne pepper and thyme.

2) Meanwhile, cook the pasta until *al dente*. Drain and toss with the sauce. Season with salt, and serve with grated cheese.

Spaghettini with Asparagus and Capers

This excellent pasta is wonderful when the asparagus season is upon us. It's nice to have a dish with asparagus that isn't rich with butter, cream or cheese; rather it glistens with fragrant olive oil and tangy tomatoes. Adding capers at the last minute gives the salty accent usually provided by the richer grated cheese. Spaghettini is thinner, more delicate and faster to cook than spaghetti.

SERVES 4

½	onion, chopped
3–5 cloves	garlic, chopped
3–4 tbsp	olive oil
1 bunch	asparagus cut into bite-sized pieces, tough ends broken off
400 g/14 oz/2⅓ cups	tomatoes (tinned is fine, include the juices)
350 g/12 oz	spaghettini
	sea salt and freshly ground black pepper to taste
pinch	of oregano
2–3 tsp	salt-preserved capers, or ordinary bottled capers, well-rinsed and dried

1) Lightly sauté the onion and half the garlic in the olive oil until softened, then add the asparagus and tomatoes. Cook over a high heat until the tomatoes reduce to a sauce-like consistency and the asparagus is just cooked. Remove from the heat.
2) Cook the pasta until *al dente,* then drain and toss with the sauce. Season with salt, pepper, oregano and capers. Serve right away.

Three-coloured Pasta
with Tomato-Garlic Sauce

If you cannot find three-coloured pasta, use plain pasta of any chunky shape. Diced vegetables, of nearly any persuasion, can be included in this pasta. Sometimes I add sautéed diced aubergine just before serving; at other times diced courgettes (zucchini), peas or fennel.

SERVES 4

500 g/1 lb	three-coloured pasta shells or other shapes
6–8 garlic cloves,	coarsely chopped
3 tbsp	extra virgin olive oil
1 kg/2½ lb/6 cups	ripe tomatoes, diced or
600–750 g/18–20 oz/2½–3⅓ cups	tinned, including the juices
	salt and coarsely ground black pepper, to taste
pinch	of sugar
5–6	large basil leaves, thinly sliced
	freshly grated Parmesan cheese, as desired

1) Cook the pasta until *al dente*.
2) Warm the garlic in the olive oil until fragrant and just beginning to colour. Add the tomatoes. Cook over a medium to high heat for 8–10 minutes or until thick and sauce-like (tinned tomatoes will take less time, fresh longer). Season with salt, pepper and sugar.
3) Drain the pasta and toss it with the tomato sauce.
4) Serve sprinkled with basil and Parmesan.

Variation for Leftovers

Layer the pasta with goat's cheese or ricotta cheese, Parmesan and peas, ending with a layer of Parmesan. Bake in a medium-hot oven for 15–20 minutes or long enough to heat the casserole through and lightly gratinée the top. Serve right away.

Pasta e Verdure Miste

Combining two different shapes of pasta with two different green vegetables is typical Italian with and whimsy. It also makes a variety of tastes and textures in each bite. The round circles of ditalini and peas, next to the lines and squiggles of spaghetti and green beans, make an almost abstract design of this simple pasta dish. When there is a small amount of this pasta and that one, Italian homemakers or shopkeepers will often put them in a jar, and the next time there is a little extra of a different shape, in the jar it goes as well. Soon you have a collection of different shapes and sizes, which add delight when eaten as is or added to soups.

SERVES 4

5 cloves	garlic, thinly sliced
3 tbsp	extra virgin olive oil
1 kg/2½ lb/6 cups	ripe tomatoes, diced or 16–18 oz tinned tomatoes, diced, including their juices
	salt and freshly ground black pepper to taste
pinch	of sugar
½ tsp	oregano leaves, or to taste
175–250 g/6–8 oz	ditalini or other small, short, elbow pasta or round macaroni
175–250 g/6–8 oz	spaghetti
250 g/8 oz	thin green beans, topped and tailed and cut into bite-sized lengths
4–6 tbsp	blanched fresh peas or frozen peas

1) Heat the garlic in the olive oil until it lightly colours, then add the tomatoes and cook over a medium-high heat, stirring with a wooden spoon, until it thickens and concentrates into a sauce-like mixture. This will take only about 5 minutes if using tinned tomatoes, and about 15 if using fresh.

2) Season with salt, pepper, sugar and oregano.

3) Meanwhile, cook the ditalini and spaghetti until almost *al dente*, then add the green beans and peas and continue to cook until the vegetables are bright green and crisp-tender and the pasta is *al dente*.

4) Drain, and toss with the sauce. Serve right away.

Paglia e Fieno al Aurora

Paglia e fieno means straw and hay, a nickname for the classic combination of yellow and green pasta, as the colours are reminiscent of the yellow haystacks and green piles of straw so much a part of the Tuscan landscape. The term *aurora* refers to a favourite local sauce of tomato and cream.

If I felt very ambitious, I might make an aubergine (eggplant) dish as well, or perhaps Verdure Arrosti (*see Chapter 6, page 134*).

SERVES 4–6

1	small onion, chopped
4 cloves	garlic, chopped
250 g/8 oz/3 cups	cultivated mushrooms, chopped
30 g/1 oz	butter
750 g/1½ lb/4½ cups	ripe tomatoes, diced or 400 g/14 oz/1¾ cups tinned diced tomatoes, including the juices
30 g/1 oz	tomato purée
250–350 ml/8–12 fl oz/ 1–1½ cups	double cream
175 g/6 oz/1 cup	fresh and blanched or frozen green peas (young petits pois are best)
	salt and freshly ground black pepper, to taste
250 g/8 oz	yellow fettucine
250 g/8 oz	green fettucine
handful	of sweet basil leaves, cut into strips or several tbsp coarsely chopped fresh marjoram
	freshly grated Parmesan, to taste

1) Lightly sauté the onion, garlic and mushrooms in the butter until just softened. Add the tomatoes and tomato purée and cook over a medium heat until thick and sauce-like. This will take longer with fresh tomatoes; no time at all with tinned.

2) Stir in the cream and continue to cook over a medium-high heat for another 10 minutes or so, or until the flavours have combined and the sauce has thickened again. Add the peas, then season with salt and pepper.

3) Meanwhile, cook the pasta until *al dente*, then drain. Serve immediately, tossed with the sauce and sprinkled with the basil or marjoram and Parmesan. Offer more Parmesan for eaters to sprinkle on as desired.

Pasta Arrabbiata

Arrabbiata means angry, in this case 'angry' with hot pepper. A good *arrabbiata* sauce can either grab your throat with its fiery heat, or merely warm you gently, whichever you prefer. It should also, to my taste at least, fairly reek with garlic.

The cheese topping is optional – sometimes I choose it; other times the spicy sauce seems tastiest and lighter without it.

SERVES 4

1–2	dried hot chilli peppers, broken into several pieces or crumbled into flakes
6 garlic cloves,	thinly sliced or chopped
3 tbsp	extra virgin olive oil
340–400 ml/12–14 fl oz/ 1½ cups	tomato passata
	salt and freshly ground black pepper to taste
a pinch	of sugar, to balance the tomatoes' acidity
375 g/12 oz pasta of choice:	bucatini (thick, long strands of macaroni), vermicelli, fettucine, spaghetti, conchiglie, etc.
3 tbsp	chopped parsley, preferably flat-leaf
	freshly grated Parmesan, as desired

1) Warm the chilli peppers and garlic in the olive oil until the garlic is fragrant but not browned. As always when heating chilli peppers in oil, take care not to inhale the irritating fumes.

2) Add the tomato passata. Season with salt, pepper and sugar, then cook the sauce for 5–10 minutes or long enough for the flavours to combine and bloom.

3) Cook the pasta until *al dente,* then drain.
4) Toss the drained pasta with the sauce and sprinkle with the parsley then serve right away, with the Parmesan if desired.

Pasta with Greens and Cherry Tomatoes

This rustic, peasant fare is deliciously satisfying and healthy too. Serve following a selection of little *antipasti*, as energetic a selection as you can put together. Barring that, open a jar or two and arrange a few olives on a plate.

SERVES 4

750 g/1½ lb	greens such as kale, broccoli tops (broccoli di rape or rabe), spinach, turnip tops, etc.
500 g/1 lb	orecchiette or little ear pasta (small, round, slightly bowl shaped)
4–6 tbsp	extra virgin olive oil
3 cloves	garlic, chopped
15–20	ripe cherry tomatoes, halved
	salt and freshly ground black pepper or red (cayenne) pepper, to taste
	freshly grated or shaved Parmesan or pecorino, to taste

1) Cook the greens in boiling salted water for 3–4 minutes, then add the pasta and cook together until the pasta is *al dente* and the greens are just tender. Drain and toss the pasta and greens with 1 tbsp of the olive oil.
2) Meanwhile, heat the remaining oil with the garlic, then quickly sauté the tomatoes over medium to high heat for 3–5 minutes.
3) Combine the pasta and greens with the sautéed tomatoes and serve immediately, seasoned with salt and either black or red (cayenne) pepper, and toss with Parmesan cheese.

Pasta con Zucchini

This dish comes from the island of Capri, and is delightful in its unfashionably simmered courgettes (zucchini) – instead of being crisp-tender they are soft and melt into the tomato sauce.

SERVES 4

3–5 cloves	garlic, chopped
2 tbsp	extra virgin olive oil
250 ml/8 fl oz/1 cup	tomato passata
3–4	small to medium courgettes (zucchini), cut into bite-sized chunks or thick slices
375 g/12 oz pasta of choice:	chunky pasta such as shells, round macaroni, rigatoni, etc. or long strands such as spaghetti or fettucine, or very thin pasta such as cappellini freshly grated Parmesan or pecorino cheese, to serve
handful	of fresh herbs: chopped parsley, basil, thyme, rosemary, marjoram, as desired

1) Lightly sauté the garlic in the olive oil until fragrant but not browned. Add the tomato passata and the courgettes (zucchini). Cover and simmer until the courgettes (zucchini) are falling apart (10–15 minutes), adding water or a little vegetable stock to maintain a sauce-like consistency as it cooks, if needed.

2) Cook the pasta until *al dente*, then drain.

3) Serve the pasta tossed with the sauce and sprinkled with Parmesan or pecorino cheese and herbs.

Pasta with Creamy Artichoke Sauce

This is a quick dish if you are using ready-prepared artichoke hearts, but time-consuming when made with fresh artichoke hearts (unless you are quick and nimble with your trimming fingers). Frozen artichokes are very convenient though not often available. If you cannot find them, use tinned artichoke hearts, rinsed well to rid them of their tinning brine. Do not use marinated artichoke hearts for this.

Serve following a selection of several *antipasti*; if you have little time, just slice a fresh fennel and sweet red pepper, garnish with black olives, and dress with olive oil and lemon juice.

SERVES 4

350 g/12 oz	frozen artichoke hearts, defrosted or tinned artichoke hearts, rinsed or 3–4 fresh artichoke hearts, blanched
1	small onion, chopped
1 clove	garlic, chopped
30 g/1 oz	butter
125 ml/4 fl oz/½ cup	vegetable stock
250–300 ml/8–10 fl oz/ 1–1⅓ cups	double cream
pinch	of cayenne pepper or freshly ground black pepper, to taste
500 g/1 lb	fresh fettuccine or 350 g/12 oz dried freshly grated Parmesan or pecorino cheese

1) Dice the artichoke hearts and lightly sauté them with the onion and garlic in the butter, until the onions are softened.
2) Add the stock and bring to the boil, then let it simmer for 5–8 minutes or until the artichokes are quite tender. Add the cream and taste for seasoning. Salt is unlikely to be needed as stock is quite salty, but a pinch of cayenne or black pepper is called for. Cover and keep it warm while you cook the pasta.
3) Cook the pasta until *al dente*, then drain and toss with the sauce. Serve immediately, sprinkled generously with Parmesan or pecorino.

Pappardelle with Sage and Black Olives

Nuggets of salty black olives punctuate the delicacy of garlic-buttered wide noodles, while fresh sage adds flavour to this simple summer dish.

SERVES 4

375 g/12 oz	pappardelle or lasagnette, or other wide noodles
30 g/1 oz	unsalted butter, softened
1 tbsp	extra virgin olive oil
3–4 cloves	garlic, chopped
1–2 tbsp	fresh sage leaves, coarsely chopped
about 15	wrinkled black Italian olives (Gaeta) or other tasty Mediterranean black olives, stoned and halved
	salt and freshly ground black pepper, to taste
3 tbsp	freshly grated Parmesan cheese

1) Cook the pasta until *al dente*.
2) Meanwhile, mix the butter with the olive oil and garlic.
3) Drain the pasta, then return it to the pan and toss with the butter, sage and olives over a low to medium heat so that the pasta stays nice and hot and the butter melts evenly throughout the noodles.
4) Serve right away, seasoned with salt and pepper, and sprinkled with Parmesan.

Orecchiette with Tomato-rocket Sauce

This is also delicious with spaghetti or other stringy pasta in place of the chunks of orecchiette. Do try to use the older specimens of rocket for this sauce: it is more flavourful and peppery than the young, delicate stuff. Buy it at Cypriot markets, where it is sold as *rocca* or *rokka*.

SERVES 4

500 g/1 lb	orecchiette, cavatieddi or a long, stringy pasta such as spaghetti
125–185 g/4–6 oz/1⅓–2 cups	coarsely chopped rocket (arugula), or a big bunch of rocca
6–8	shallots or 3–4 cloves garlic, chopped (or use both)
2–3 tbsp	extra virgin olive oil
500 g/1 lb/3 cups	fresh ripe tomatoes, chopped or diced, mixed with 1 tbsp tomato purée or 500 g/16 oz/2¼ cups tinned diced tomatoes
pinch	of sugar
	salt and cayenne pepper or red chilli flakes, to taste

1) Cook the pasta until almost *al dente*. Add the rocket, cook for a few moments longer, then drain.
2) Meanwhile, lightly sauté the shallots and/or garlic in the olive oil then add the tomatoes and a pinch of sugar. Cook over a high heat until the sauce thickens, then season with salt and cayenne or hot pepper flakes.
3) Toss the pasta and rocket with the tomato sauce and serve right away.

Spaghetti con le Noci

Spaghetti and toasted hazelnuts make a delicious combination.
Serve with a starter of Antipasto of Grilled Vegetables and Pesto
(*see Chapter 1, page 11*).

SERVES 4

90–125 g/3–4 oz/¾ cup	shelled hazelnuts
4–5 cloves	garlic, chopped
60 ml/2 fl oz/¼ cup	extra virgin olive oil
350 g/12 oz	spaghetti
1 tbsp	fresh thyme leaves or ¼–½ tsp dried thyme
	freshly ground black pepper, to taste
30 g/1 oz/½ cup	freshly grated Parmesan or pecorino cheese
	fresh parsley, chopped, to serve

1) Toast the hazelnuts in a heavy ungreased frying pan over a medium heat, turning them frequently to prevent burning. They should become flecked with dark brown. When they are nearly ready their skins will split and begin to fall off. Alternatively, hazelnuts may be roasted in the oven at 200°C/400°F/gas mark 6 for about 10 minutes.

2) Place the toasted hazelnuts in a clean towel and rub them together, letting the nuts rub each other until their skins fall off into the towel.

3) In a blender or food processor, finely chop the garlic then add the hazelnuts and process them to a coarse, mealy texture. Add enough olive oil to make a thinnish paste, then set them aside.

4) Cook the pasta until *al dente*, then drain. Toss the pasta with the hazelnut paste and the thyme, and season with the pepper. Add a little more olive oil if the nut paste is too thick.

5) Serve immediately, seasoned with black pepper and sprinkled with lots of Parmesan or pecorino and parsley.

Capellini with Peas, Porcini and Tomatoes

This is very nice, though slightly naughty, when prepared with butter instead of olive oil. If you are feeling lazier or if time is even more iffy than usual, break the mushrooms into small pieces and add directly to the sauce, eliminating the soak. The only drawback to this is that you could end up with grit getting into the sauce.

SERVES 4

15 g/½ oz/½ cup	dried porcini
185 ml/6 fl oz/¾ cup	very hot but not boiling vegetable stock or water
1	small onion, coarsely chopped
2 cloves	garlic, chopped
2 tbsp	extra virgin olive oil
8	ripe tomatoes, diced plus 1 tbsp tomato purée, or 400 g/14 oz/2⅓ cups diced tomatoes (tinned is fine)
	salt and freshly ground black pepper, to taste
pinch	of sugar, to balance tomatoes' acidity
350 g/12 oz	capellini
125 g/4 oz/1¼ cups	fresh young peas, blanched or frozen petits pois
8–10	fresh basil leaves, thinly sliced
	freshly grated Parmesan or pecorino cheese

1) Combine the porcini with the hot stock or water in a bowl with a tight-fitting lid. Leave to rehydrate while you prepare the sauce.

2) Lightly sauté the onion and garlic in about two-thirds of the olive oil until softened. Remove the porcini from its soaking liquid, chop it coarsely, then add it to the onion and garlic. Cook and stir for a few moments, then add the tomatoes and tomato purée or the tinned tomatoes, salt, pepper and sugar. Simmer over a medium-low heat.

3) Meanwhile, strain the soaking liquid to rid it of its grit. Pour the strained liquid into the tomato mixture then raise the heat and cook over a medium-high heat for about 10 minutes or long enough for the sauce to cook down into a flavourful mixture.

4) Cook the pasta until *al dente*, then drain and toss with the peas and tomato sauce. Serve sprinkled with the basil and Parmesan or pecorino cheese.

Ditalini with Fennel and Peas

Fresh fennel is delicious in this dish. If you do not have it, the fennel seeds alone give a very anise-y flavour, though you could add a little diced celery if you liked, for texture.

SERVES 4

2	onions, chopped
4 cloves	garlic, chopped
2 tbsp	either butter, extra virgin olive oil, or a combination of both
1 bulb	fennel, diced, including the wispy fronds and leaves (if no fresh fennel is available, just omit or use a stalk of celery, diced)
2 tbsp	chopped parsley, preferably flat-leaf
250 g/8 oz/1½ cups	fresh or frozen young peas
500 ml/16 fl oz/2¼ cups	vegetable stock or water mixed with a stock cube
Large pinch	each of mixed dried herbs and fennel seeds
375 g/12 oz	ditalini, elbows or other short pasta
	salt and freshly ground black pepper, to taste
	freshly grated Parmesan cheese, to serve

1) Lightly sauté the onions and garlic in the butter and/or olive oil until just softened.
2) Add the fennel (or celery), parsley and peas, and cook for a few minutes until the fennel is softened and the parsley and peas are bright green, then add the stock. Cook over a high heat until the liquid is reduced to only a few tbsp and has a very intense flavour.
3) Add the herbs and fennel seeds and set the sauce aside.
4) Meanwhile, cook the pasta until *al dente*, then drain. Toss the pasta with the pea sauce, season with salt and pepper, then serve sprinkled generously with Parmesan.

Spaghetti with Peas and Lusty Tomato Sauce

Peas simmered with tomatoes and herbs make a hearty, lusty tomato sauce that is good with nearly any shaped pasta, though I like it best with ordinary spaghetti. As always, be sure that the quality of your spaghetti is high. Excellent spaghetti, made in Italy of good strong durum wheat, chewy and wholesome, is to my mind far superior to many fresh pastas.

SERVES 4

1	small onion, chopped
3 cloves	garlic, chopped
2 tbsp	extra virgin olive oil
1 kg/2½ lb/6½ cups	ripe tomatoes, diced or 2 tins (400 g/14 oz/ 1¾ cups each)
2 tbsp	tomato purée
pinch	of sugar
½ tsp	dried mixed herbs or thyme, or to taste
¼ tsp	fennel seeds, or more to taste
	salt and freshly ground black pepper, to taste
375 g/12 oz/2½ cups	fresh young peas or frozen peas
250–500 g/12–16 oz	spaghetti
handful	of chopped fresh parsley or basil
	freshly grated Parmesan cheese, to serve

1) Lightly sauté the onion and garlic in the olive oil until soft and translucent (about 7 minutes). Add the tomatoes, tomato purée, sugar, herbs or thyme, fennel, salt and pepper. Cook over a medium-high heat for about 10 minutes or until the sauce is thickened.

2) Add the peas, and continue to stir and cook until the peas are just cooked or heated through and tender, and the sauce is flavourful. Add herbs, fennel, salt and pepper as desired.

3) Cook the spaghetti until *al dente*, then drain. Toss with the pea and tomato sauce, then serve right away, sprinkled with parsley or basil and Parmesan.

Orzo Pasta with Peas, Cream and Saffron

Because of its slightly soupy consistency, serve this rich dish in soup bowls with spoons rather than forks.

A light and vivacious salad, such as Orange, Fennel and Green Olive Salad (*see Chapter 2, page 21*), would make a refreshing counterpoint to the richness of this dish.

SERVES 4

375 g/12 oz	orzo or other small melon-seed shaped pasta
4 cloves	garlic, chopped
45 g/1½ oz	butter
500 ml/16 fl oz/2¼ cups	vegetable stock (or water mixed with a vegetable stock cube)
285 ml/10 fl oz/1⅓ cups	single cream
1–2 tbsp	Greek yoghurt or crème fraîche (optional)
250 g/8 oz/1½ cups	peas, preferably petits pois, either fresh and blanched or frozen
large pinch	of saffron threads, dissolved in 1 tbsp cold water
	freshly grated Parmesan cheese, for sprinkling generously

1) Cook the orzo until almost but not quite *al dente* – it should still have a slightly crunchy heart. Drain and set aside.
2) Lightly heat the garlic in the butter until just fragrant but not browned, then add the stock and the cooked orzo. Heat until bubbly around the edges.
3) Stir in the cream, the yoghurt or crème fraîche if using, the peas and saffron. Heat together, stirring well until smooth and creamy. It should be soupy but thickened.
4) Serve right away, topping each portion with a generous sprinkling of Parmesan.

Tomatoey Pasta with Broccoli and Ricotta Cheese

Robust chewy pasta, served up with fennel-scented tomato sauce, punctuated with nuggets of broccoli and dollops of snowy ricotta cheese.

SERVES 4–6

4–6 cloves	garlic, chopped
1–2	small onions, chopped
1	small carrot, diced
2 tbsp	extra virgin olive oil
1½ tsp	fennel seeds
1 tsp	chopped fresh marjoram or oregano
several pinches	of dried thyme
750 g/1½ lb/4½ cups	fresh ripe tomatoes, chopped or 1½ tins (400-g/14-oz/1¾-cup tins) diced tomatoes
3 tbsp	tomato purée
	salt and freshly ground black pepper, to taste
pinch	of sugar
500 g/1 lb	chunky pasta such as rotelle, penne or rigatoni
1 large or 2 small	head(s) broccoli, broken into bite-sized florets, stems peeled and diced
2 tbsp	chopped fresh rosemary or 3 tbsp chopped fresh basil
250 g/8 oz	fresh ricotta cheese
	freshly grated Parmesan or pecorino, to taste

1) Lightly sauté the garlic, onion and carrot in the olive oil until softened, then add the fennel, marjoram or oregano, thyme, tomatoes and tomato purée. Cook over a medium-high heat, stirring every so often, until the mixture is thickened and sauce-like. It should take about 5–8 minutes for tinned tomatoes, 10–15 minutes for fresh.
2) Season with salt, pepper and sugar.
3) Meanwhile, cook the pasta until *al dente*. When it is half-cooked, add the broccoli and continue to cook until the pasta is *al dente*, the vegetables bright green and crisp-tender. Drain well.
4) Toss the pasta and broccoli with the tomato sauce, and serve sprinkled with the rosemary or basil, the ricotta and Parmesan or pecorino.

Conchiglie con Melanzane

Sometimes I add green beans in addition to or instead of the aubergine (eggplant) to this dish of shell-shaped pasta.

SERVES 4–6

1	aubergine (eggplant), diced or cut into bite-sized cubes
60 ml/2 fl oz/¼ cup	extra virgin olive oil, or more as desired
	salt and freshly ground black pepper, to taste
1	onion, coarsely chopped
4 cloves	garlic, chopped
1	yellow sweet pepper, diced
400 g/14 oz/2⅓ cups	diced tomatoes (tinned are fine)
pinch	of sugar, if needed
1 tsp	chopped fresh marjoram, or ½ tsp dried oregano leaves
350 g/12 oz	shell-shaped pasta
	freshly grated Parmesan or pecorino, to taste

1) Brown the aubergine (eggplant) in a few tbsp of the olive oil; season with salt when they are lightly browned. Set aside.
2) Meanwhile, sauté the onion, garlic and yellow pepper in the rest of the olive oil until softened, about 5–8 minutes. Add the tomatoes, salt, pepper and sugar and cook over a medium-high heat until thick and sauce-like. Add the marjoram or oregano.
3) Cook the pasta until *al dente*. Toss with the sauce, then with the aubergine (eggplant).
4) Serve right away, sprinkled with Parmesan or pecorino.

Spaghetti alla Norma

The name of this classic pasta and aubergine (eggplant) dish of Sicily is a result of the island's passion for its native composer Bellini. His famous opera *Norma* was such a resounding success that 'Norma' became a term of excellence, and anything wonderful in nearly any sphere of life was called 'alla Norma'.

In Sicily you can buy the aubergines (eggplants) already fried in the markets. However, I find that it saves not only time, but calories and fat as well, to brush the aubergine (eggplant) with olive oil then grill it.

SERVES 4

2	large aubergines (eggplants), sliced crossways into ⅛–¼ inch/3–6 mm thick slices
	extra virgin olive oil
	salt as desired
1	onion, chopped
3 cloves	garlic, chopped
pinch	of sugar
570 ml/1 pint/2½ cups	tomato passata or 850 g/2 lb/5 cups ripe tomatoes, diced or 2 tins diced tomatoes (400 g/14 oz/1¾ cups each)
	freshly ground black pepper, to taste
500 g/1 lb	spaghetti
handful	of fresh herbs such as basil, marjoram, oregano, parsley, thyme, etc.
	freshly grated ricotta salata cheese, Parmesan or pecorino, as desired

1) Preheat the grill.
2) Brush the aubergine (eggplant) slices with olive oil, sprinkle with salt, and grill on both sides until lightly browned and just tender. Remove from the heat.
3) Meanwhile, lightly sauté the onion and garlic in olive oil until softened, then sprinkle in a pinch of sugar and cook for a moment. Stir in the passata or diced tomatoes, season with salt and black pepper, and cook over a medium-high heat until slightly thickened and flavourful. It should taste of rich tomatoes – the herbs will get scattered on at the end of cooking.
4) Cook the pasta until *al dente*, then drain.
5) Mound the spaghetti on a platter, then spoon on the sauce and surround the spaghetti and sauce with the sliced browned aubergines (eggplants). Sprinkle the top generously with the herbs and cheese and serve right away.

Pasta from the Garden

Serve this dish as a main course, with Asparagus and Eggs with Truffle Oil (*see Chapter 6, page 143*) as a starter.

SERVES 4

3	spring onions, thinly sliced
2 cloves	garlic, chopped
1 tbsp	chopped parsley
3 tbsp	butter
2	small to medium or 1 large courgette (zucchini), diced
4	artichoke hearts, cut into bite-sized pieces (blanched; frozen is fine; tinned is fine if rinsed well in cold water) or asparagus spears, cut into bite-sized pieces
175 g/6 oz/1 cup	peas (fresh young peas, blanched, or frozen petits pois)
8–10	ripe tomatoes, diced (fresh is really best here)
1–2 tbsp	tomato purée
pinch	of sugar
	salt and freshly ground black pepper, to taste
500 g/1 lb	spaghetti or other pasta of choice
	freshly grated Parmesan, pecorino or similar grating cheese, to serve
handful	of fresh herbs: marjoram, basil, parsley, rosemary, or whatever is available

1) Gently sauté the spring onions, garlic and parsley in half the butter until softened, then add the courgettes (zucchini) and artichoke hearts and cook gently for about 5 minutes.

2) Add the peas, tomatoes and tomato purée, plus about 60–90 ml/2–3 fl oz/¼–⅓ cup of water and cook over a medium-high heat for another few minutes until the mixture has the consistency – and taste – of a sauce.

3) Season with sugar, salt and pepper and set aside.

4) Cook the pasta until *al dente*, then drain. Toss the pasta with the remaining butter then with the sauce. Serve immediately, sprinkled with the cheese and herbs.

Linguine alla Pizzaiola

Classic flavours of the Italian summertime: tomatoes, mozzarella and basil. Serve lightly toasted country bread spread with Ligurian Black Olive Paste (*see Chapter 1, page 4*) to begin with.

SERVES 4–6

3 cloves	garlic, coarsely chopped
3 tbsp	extra virgin olive oil
10	ripe, sweet tomatoes, diced (tinned diced tomatoes are acceptable)
2 tbsp	tomato purée
	salt and freshly ground black pepper to taste
a pinch	of sugar
350–500 g/12–16 oz	linguine
250–350 g/8–12 oz/1½–2 cups	fresh milky mozzarella cheese (about 2 balls), diced or cut into small bite-sized pieces
several handfuls	of fresh basil leaves, coarsely torn or left whole

1) Warm the garlic in the olive oil to bring out its fragrance. Add the tomatoes and tomato purée and cook for a minute or two over a medium-high heat, adding a little water if needed to prevent burning. Season with salt, pepper and sugar, and keep simmering at a low heat while you cook the pasta.

2) Cook the linguine until *al dente*, then drain and toss the pasta with the hot sauce and scatter then toss with the mozzarella cheese. Serve with the basil sprinkled generously over the top, and eat right away, before the mozzarella has had a chance to cool into hard, gluey chunks.

Pasta with Vegetables, Cheese and Breadcrumbs

This variation on a traditional mountain dish from the Italian Alps is hearty indeed, and can be varied endlessly. Cabbage and asparagus are two of my other vegetable choices, but I'll choose green beans when in season – their crunch is quite delightful with the richness of the pasta and sauce.

SERVES 4–6

125 g/4 oz/2 cups	breadcrumbs, preferably homemade or fresh ones or 2–3 slices country bread such as ciabatta, grated over the large holes of a grater into coarse crumbs
1 tbsp	extra virgin olive oil or butter
500 g/1 lb	pasta shapes of choice: I like medium-sized fat seashell shapes, farfalle (bow ties) or pasta gnocchi shapes
250 g/8 oz	green beans, topped and tailed, and cut into bite-sized pieces
340 ml/12 fl oz/1½ cups	vegetable stock (or water mixed with ½ stock cube)
155–250 g/5–8 oz	mascarpone cheese, at room temperature
175 g/6 oz	fontina or Gruyère cheese, coarsely grated
2–3 tbsp	coarsely grated Parmesan or pecorino salt and freshly ground black pepper, to taste

1) Toast the breadcrumbs in the oil or butter in a heavy frying pan over a low to medium heat until crisp and golden (about 5 minutes). Remove from the heat and set aside.
2) Cook the pasta until half-cooked, then add the green beans and continue to cook until both are *al dente*; drain.
3) Meanwhile, heat the stock until it bubbles around the edges then add the breadcrumbs and mascarpone cheese. Stir until the cheese melts creamily into the sauce, then toss the sauce with the pasta and green beans, and toss with the fontina or Gruyère and the Parmesan or pecorino. Season with salt and pepper and serve right away.

Pappardelle with Broccoli and Red Beans

Wide noodles, tossed with a brash and satisfying mixture of broccoli, tomatoes and red beans, is a typical dish from the Mezzogiorno, or Italy's sun-drenched south. Any fairly large pasta shape is good with this hearty and wholesome sauce – I especially like the hollow tubes called bucatini, and often add a shake of red hot peppers when I use this shape.

SERVES 4–6

3–4 cloves	garlic, chopped
3 tbsp	extra virgin olive oil
2 small heads or 1 large head	of broccoli, cut into florets, the stems peeled and diced
5	fresh ripe or 6 tinned tomatoes, diced, with the juices
340 ml/12 fl oz/1½ cups	tomato passata
pinch	of sugar
	salt and freshly ground black pepper, to taste
400 g/14 oz/2⅓ cups	cooked or tinned red kidney beans, drained
500 g/1 lb	pappardelle or other pasta shape of choice
	freshly grated Parmesan cheese, to taste

1) Lightly sauté the garlic in the olive oil until the garlic is fragrant and barely coloured, then add the broccoli and cook over a medium heat for a minute or two. Add the tomatoes and tomato passata and continue to cook for about 5 minutes over a high heat. Season with sugar, salt and pepper, lower the heat to a simmer and cook until thickened (about 5 more minutes).
2) Add the beans to the broccoli and sauce and continue to simmer while you cook the pasta.
3) Cook the pappardelle until *al dente*, then drain carefully so that the big fat noodles do not fall apart.
4) Serve the pasta tossed with the broccoli and red bean tomato sauce, blanketed with a generous grating of Parmesan.

Tortellini and Courgettes (Zucchini) with Lemon

On a hot, sultry day this makes a marvellous lunch, taking very little in the way of energy expenditure, but able to put a smile on even the most recalcitrant of faces.

SERVES 4

3–4	medium-sized courgettes (zucchini), cut into thick slices or chunks
12 oz	ricotta cheese and/or vegetable-stuffed tortellini or ravioli
1–2 tbsp	extra virgin olive oil
juice	of 1 lemon or lime
	freshly ground black pepper, to taste
90–125 g/3–4 oz/1½–2 cups	(about 8 tbsp) Parmesan cheese, freshly grated

1) Cook the courgettes (zucchini) in rapidly boiling salted water until half-cooked, then add the pasta and continue to cook until the pasta is *al dente*, about 3–4 minutes depending on the type of pastas you are using.
2) Drain, toss with the olive oil, lemon or lime juice, black pepper and Parmesan. Serve right away, or eat it at room temperature.

Ravioli with Crisp-fried Sage

Frying fresh young sage leaves crisps them up deliciously, leaving the oil or butter they cooked in fragrant and tasty. I like the addition of a little tomato to lighten the sage-scented oil.

SERVES 4–6

25–30	fresh young sage leaves (they must be fresh)
5 tbsp	olive oil
500 g/1 lb	cheese- or vegetable-filled ravioli
	salt and freshly ground black pepper, to taste
4–6	ripe tomatoes, diced
2 tbsp passata	
2–3 tbsp	freshly grated Parmesan or pecorino

1) Fry the sage leaves in the olive oil until just crisp. Remove from the heat and set aside.

2) Cook the ravioli until *al dente*, then drain.

3) Drizzle the oil and sage leaves over the hot ravioli, then season with salt and pepper.

4) Stir together the tomatoes and passata and spoon over the ravioli. Serve sprinkled with the cheese.

Spinach Ravioli
with Summer Vegetables

Spinach- and ricotta-filled ravioli, tossed with whatever fresh vegetables your summer garden has on offer, is a delicious, endlessly variable dish. Make it with the changing vegetables of the season, and with the wide variety of ravioli and other stuffed pasta available these days.

I might serve Aubergine (Eggplant) Rolls Stuffed with Cheese (*see Chapter 1, page 17*), as either a starter or a main course.

SERVES 4–6

90–125 ml/3–4 oz/³⁄₄–1 cup	sugar snap peas
2	summer squash, either courgettes (zucchini) or yellow courgettes (zucchini), or small pale-green or yellow turban-shaped squashes, cut into bite-sized pieces
10–15	leaves of chard (silver beet) or spinach, cut into thin ribbons
5	sun-dried tomatoes (the dried rather than the marinated ones), cut into strips (optional)
3 cloves	garlic, chopped
4–5 tbsp	extra virgin olive oil
handful	of fresh basil leaves, thinly sliced
350 g/12 oz	spinach ravioli, or other stuffed pasta, as desired
	salt and freshly ground black pepper
60 g/2 oz/1 cup	freshly grated Parmesan cheese

1) Blanch the vegetables, including the sun-dried tomatoes if using. Set them aside. They may be done together and should take about 3–4 minutes.
2) Drain the water into the pot for cooking the pasta.
3) Sauté the garlic in the olive oil until golden, then add the blanched vegetables and toss briefly, then add the basil and set aside.
4) Meanwhile heat the water for the pasta, adding more hot water to fill the pan until you have the required amount of water. Cook the ravioli until *al dente*. Drain.
5) Toss the hot pasta with the warm vegetables and serve right away, seasoned with salt and pepper and sprinkled generously with Parmesan.

Gnocchi with Green Beans and Gorgonzola

This rich and luxurious dish is laughingly simple and quick to prepare. Serve a light salad or *antipasto* as a first course, something like roasted peppers (*see La Dispensa*/The Store Cupboard, *page xvii*), or Sautéed Mushrooms with Salad Leaves (*see Chapter 2, page 32*).

SERVES 4

1	packet gnocchi
175–250 g/6–8 oz	thin green beans, topped and tailed and cut into bite-sized lengths
175 g/6 oz	Gorgonzola cheese, cut into small pieces
1 tbsp	fresh basil or sage leaves, cut into thin strips

1) Cook the gnocchi in rapidly boiling salted water until tender, about 5 minutes or according to packet directions. During the last minute or two of cooking, add the green beans.
2) Drain carefully, then toss the cooked gnocchi and beans with the Gorgonzola and sage. Serve right away.

Gnocchi 'Brutto ma Buono'

'Brutto ma buono' means 'ugly but good'. The ugly part comes about because sautéed mushrooms are lumpy, brown and not particularly pretty to look at. The good refers to its deliciousness of course. I often serve asparagus with it as a beautiful green complement.

Choose any selection of less-than-usual mushrooms, especially fresh ceps or porcini if they are available. Otherwise, sauté up ordinary cultivated mushrooms and add a tiny handful of dried porcini to oomph up the foresty flavour.

SERVES 4

500 g/1 lb/6 cups	mushrooms, thinly sliced (choose either common cultivated ones or exotic mushrooms such as ceps/porcini, oyster, fairy ring, etc.)
2–3 tbsp	butter or olive oil, or as desired
½	red onion or 3 shallots, chopped
3 cloves	garlic, chopped
250 ml/8 fl oz/1 cup	vegetable stock
several tbsp	dried mushrooms, such as porcini, fairy ring, etc., broken into small pieces (omit if using exotic mushrooms instead of cultivated ones)
a grating	of nutmeg, to taste
	salt and freshly ground black pepper
1 packet	gnocchi
	Parmesan cheese, in shavings

1) Sauté the mushrooms in the butter or olive oil with the onion or shallots and garlic for a few minutes or until the mushrooms are lightly browned in spots. Add the stock, dried mushrooms, nutmeg, salt and pepper and cook over a high heat for 5 minutes or so, long enough to reduce and intensify the liquid and rehydrate the dried mushrooms if using. When the sauce is finished, set it aside and taste for seasoning.

2) Cook the gnocchi until just tender, then drain and toss with the sauce. Serve blanketed with the shaved Parmesan cheese.

Riso e Polenta
Rice, Risotto and Polenta

For those not eating pasta (or soup) as a first course, there is rice and polenta, both of which make excellent main courses, too.

Riso con Erbe

Steamed rice is forked through with a mixture of garlic, herbs, olive oil and lemon. It is refreshing and delicious, good alongside almost anything.

SERVES 4

3 cloves	garlic, crushed in a pestle and mortar
1 tbsp each:	chopped basil, fresh tarragon, dill, parsley, mint, rosemary
3–5 tbsp	chopped chives
1 tbsp	lemon juice
	salt and freshly ground black pepper to taste
60 ml/2 fl oz/¼ cup	extra virgin olive oil
250 g/8 oz/1¼ cups	long-grain white rice

1) Combine the crushed garlic with the fresh herbs, the chives, lemon juice, salt and pepper, then work in the olive oil. Leave to sit while you prepare the rice; this herbal mixture can be made up to a day in advance, and it gives the herbs a chance to steep.

2) Cook the rice in abundant boiling water until it is almost done but has a slightly tough centre. Drain well, then place it back in the pan, cover with a clean cloth and then with the tight-fitting lid. Cook over a very low heat for about 3–5 minutes or just long enough for the rice to cook through.

3) Remove the lid and cloth, fork the rice to fluff it up, then fork in the herbs with the olive oil. Serve right away, or let it cool and enjoy it as a salad, surrounded by ripe, sliced tomatoes.

Rice with Cabbage and Tomatoes

I love risotto-type dishes that are strongly flavoured and not necessarily rich with cheese or cream as so many can be. This one has the good, strong flavour of tomatoes and the sturdy freshness of cabbage, though any similar green, such as kale, spinach, Swiss chard, arugula (the mature kind usually sold as *roka*), can be used in its place. Instead of a sprinkling of cheese, this dish has a final enrichment of olive oil and a sprinkling of chopped parsley and garlic.

The speckles of green parsley, the drizzle of golden oil and the rich red colour of the rice makes this dish as appealing to look at as it is satisfying to eat.

SERVES 4

250 g/8 oz/1¼ cups	long-grain rice
½	medium-sized cabbage, either plain white or curly savoy, thinly sliced or shredded
1	medium to large onion, chopped
5 cloves	garlic, chopped
3 tbsp	olive oil, plus more for drizzling on at the end
	salt and freshly ground black pepper, to taste
400 g/14 oz/2⅓ cups	tomatoes, diced
175 ml/6 fl oz/¾ cup	tomato juice (if using tinned tomatoes, use the juice from the tin)
175 ml/6 fl oz/¾ cup	chicken or vegetable stock, or as needed
large pinch	of herbs of choice: sage, oregano, thyme, rosemary, or a mixture
2 tbsp	parsley, finely chopped

1) Parboil the rice until half-cooked, then drain and rinse well with cold water. Drain again and set aside. This can be done up to two days in advance and kept in the refrigerator.

2) Blanch the cabbage in boiling water until translucent (about 5 minutes) then drain and rinse well with cold water and set aside.

3) Lightly sauté the onion and half the garlic in the olive oil until softened. Season with salt and pepper then add the tomatoes and reserved cabbage and cook together in the olive oil and onions for about 5–10 minutes or until the mixture is sauce-like and the cabbage cloaked in a pale red colour. Add the tomato juice, stock and herbs and bring to the boil, then add the reserved rice, forking it in gently so as not to break the kernels (which can give a gummy result).

4) Cover and cook over a low heat for about 5 minutes or long enough to finish cooking the rice; the finished dish will be soupy, however, so don't wait until it is dry – the rice would then be overcooked.

5) Remove from the heat, fork it to fluff it a bit, then serve sprinkled with the parsley and reserved garlic, drizzled over with extra olive oil.

Risotto

Not long ago I realized how convenient a risotto was for the busy cook. I had a flatmate – Lynne Meikle – who, at the end of almost every day, walked through the door and headed for the stove and her box of risotto rice. The menu was risotto. Risotto with peas, risotto with sweetcorn, with mushrooms, with tomatoes or herbs or spinach, or, in her words, 'risotto with everything'. The rice was there, and whatever she fancied from the market was what she stirred in with it.

While not usually thought of as a quick-to-toss-together dish – it requires lots of stirring and about half an hour's cooking time – risotto is a marvellous dish to prepare at the end of a day. For one thing, all that stirring is relaxing: sip a glass of wine and mull over the day's events as the rice absorbs the liquid and plumps up deliciously. But risotto is also that rare creature: a dish that is actually wonderfully prepared in the microwave. If you have one, use it for risotto – the magic nature of the rays cooks the rice in a roundabout motion, making a risotto that has the consistency and flavour of one that has been stirred and stirred as it slow cooks.

Risotto can be as elegant as a dinner party dish, as comforting as your favourite food from childhood, as austere as rice with stock and vegetables, or as indulgent as can be, with a splodge or two of cream, a dollop of mascarpone.

Microwaving Risotto

One of the best things the microwave does is cook speedy risotto. Sauté the aromatics, such as onions and garlic, with the rice. Add the wine and stock all at once and place in the microwave. Cook for 5 minutes, remove and stir. Repeat. You should have excellent risotto in under 10 minutes. The traditional way of risotto-making takes anything from 25 minutes to 40, depending on the rice.

Risotto of Pumpkin and Red Beans

Pumpkin risotto is one of the most delicious things you can do with a pumpkin, and it is endlessly variable. Substitute white beans for the red, or omit completely; add a selection of summer squashes to go with the winter pumpkin. Omit the arugula (rocket) and spinach and top with basil, or enrich it all with a bit of cream.

SERVES 4

3 cloves	garlic
½–1	onion, chopped
4 tbsp	olive oil
300 g/11 oz/1½ cups	arborio or Italian pudding rice
350 g/12 oz	pumpkin, peeled and diced
½–1 tsp	coarsely chopped fresh marjoram, or as desired
340 ml/12 fl oz/1½ cups	dry white wine
1 litre/1¾ pints	hot vegetable stock
400 g/14oz/2⅓ cup	tin red kidney beans, drained, or cooked beans
several handfuls (1 bunch)	arugula (rocket), chard or spinach, trimmed and sliced thinly
90–125 g/3–4 oz/1½–2 cups	Parmesan, freshly grated
	salt and freshly ground pepper to taste

1) Lightly sauté the garlic and onion in the olive oil until softened, then stir in the rice and cook for a few minutes until the rice has a golden tinge. Stir in the pumpkin and marjoram, and continue to sauté over a medium-low heat for a few minutes.

2) Pour in half the white wine, raise the heat and cook, stirring, until the wine is absorbed, then add the rest of the wine and continue to cook and stir until this too is absorbed.

3) Then stir in about 125 ml/4 fl oz/½ cup of hot stock, let it absorb in the cooking. Keep stirring and repeating until the rice is cooked – about 25 minutes, depending on the rice you use. You want the rice to be *al dente*, suspended in a sauce-like mixture.

4) Add the beans and arugula (rocket) or other greens and cook only until the beans are hot and the greens are wilted and cooked.

5) Stir in about half the Parmesan, season with salt and pepper then serve, with the rest of the Parmesan for sprinkling as desired.

Risi Bisi alla Venetia

Risi bisi is one of Venice's classic dishes: soupy arborio rice dotted with tiny green peas, eaten from a soup bowl with a spoon. When the freshest young peas of spring are in the market, *risi bisi* is prepared with a stock made from simmering the pods leftover from shelling – the delicate pea flavour permeates every grain of rice when cooked.

I usually use frozen peas, though – who has time for shelling at the end of a busy day? And how often are really fresh peas in the market? You can, however, add a handful of sugar snap peas to the risotto to get added pea flavour; to gild the lily, stir a few spoonfuls of crème fraîche into the risotto.

As a variation, you can reduce the amount of rice and make this a soup dish rather than a risotto.

SERVES 4

1	onion, chopped
2 tbsp	chopped parsley, preferably flat-leaf
2 tbsp	butter
2 tbsp	olive oil
300 g/11 oz/1½ cups	arborio rice or risotto rice
250 g/8 oz/1¾ cups	shelled fresh young peas or frozen peas
1 litre/1¾ pints	hot vegetable stock or water mixed with 1–2 vegetable stock cubes
2 pinches	of saffron threads, soaked for several minutes in 1 tbsp cold water
60 g/2 oz/1 cup	Parmesan cheese, freshly grated, plus more as desired

1) Sauté the onion and parsley in the butter and olive oil until softened, then stir in the rice and cook for a few minutes, stirring as it cooks with the onions. Then stir in the peas and about 125 ml/4 fl oz/½ cup stock and cook over a medium-high heat, stirring, until the liquid is absorbed. Keep adding the liquid and stirring until the rice is *al dente* and the liquid is soupy.
2) Stir in the saffron, warm through, then stir in half the cheese and serve. You want the consistency to be like a thick soup or a thin rice dish. Serve it in bowls with the rest of the cheese sprinkled over the top.

Variation: Risotto alla Primavera/Asparagus and Pea Risotto
Young asparagus paired with peas makes a succulent spring-time risotto. Add a small bunch of young asparagus, either whole tips or stalks cut into bite-sized lengths. Stir it in about 5 minutes before the rice is *al dente*, and let it cook as the rice finishes its cooking.

LEFTOVERS
Use leftover risotto to make a gratin the next day. Smooth about half the recipe of risotto in a gratin dish with the addition of several ounces of diced cheese, such as mozzarella or tontina, then pour over it a little stock or cream. A pinch of saffron or several tbsp of chopped fresh herbs make good additions, too.

Sprinkle generously with a mixture of freshly grated Parmesan and breadcrumbs, dot with butter, and bake in a hot oven for about 20 minutes or until the top is crusty and browned. Serve very hot.

Polenta

A golden porridge of maize gruel, polenta has become very chic and trendy in recent years. When I was a child it was ladled up in bowls for breakfast, topped with melting butter and brown sugar, maybe a spoonful of sour cream. It is a bit too hefty for my breakfast regime these days, but sometimes I do stir in a few drops of vanilla essence, sweeten the cornmeal with a little sugar and milk and spoon it up to begin the day.

Polenta can be cooked with the addition of herbs such as chopped rosemary, sage or parsley, or hot peppers coarsely chopped into flakes.

Polenta alla Gorgonzola

Soft, creamy polenta, rich with melting Gorgonzola and the salty, nutty flavour of Parmesan. Sometimes I omit the basil and fry several fresh sage leaves in the butter, then pour the sage-flavoured butter over the polenta, crumble up the leaves, and sprinkle them over it as well.

SERVES 4

1 packet	instant polenta (400 g/14 oz)
3–4 heaped tbsp	mascarpone cheese or double cream
2–3 tbsp	butter, or as desired
125 g/4 oz	Gorgonzola, crumbled
2 tbsp	finely shredded basil
4–6 tbsp	freshly grated Parmesan or pecorino cheese

1) Cook the polenta according to packet instructions; this should take only about 5 minutes. Stir the mascarpone and butter into the polenta, then the Gorgonzola and basil, then serve each portion with a nugget of butter melted in and a generous sprinkling of Parmesan.

Soft Polenta with Broccoli and Tomato Sauce

Crisp, savoury broccoli stewed with tomatoes makes a delicious, hearty and mush less indulgent dinner than the previous recipe. You can even decrease the amount of olive oil to about 1 tbsp, or possibly even none, for a very low-fat dish.

SERVES 4

1	smallish onion, diced
3 cloves	garlic, chopped
3 tbsp	extra virgin olive oil
400 g/14 oz/1¾ cups	tinned diced tomatoes or 650 g/1½ lb/4 cups fresh diced tomatoes plus 1 tbsp tomato purée
1 head	of broccoli, broken into florets, the stem peeled and diced
pinch	of sugar
	salt and freshly ground black pepper, to taste
¼ tsp	mixed Italian herbs
1 packet	instant polenta (400 g/14 oz)
	freshly grated Parmesan cheese, as desired

1) Lightly sauté the onion and garlic in the olive oil until the onion is softened, then add the tomatoes and cook over a medium-high heat until sauce-like. This should take about 5 minutes if using tinned tomatoes and 10–15 minutes if using fresh.

2) Add the broccoli, sugar, salt, pepper and herbs and continue to cook for 5–10 more minutes or until the broccoli is just tender. Taste for seasoning.

3) Meanwhile, cook the polenta according to packet directions; this should take about 5 minutes.

4) Serve the soft polenta with spoonfuls of the broccoli sauce ladled over it, the whole thing blanketed with Parmesan cheese to taste.

Variation
This is tasty when made with artichoke hearts. Use quartered artichoke hearts, fresh and blanched (though this is fairly time-consuming) or frozen, or tinned and rinsed well with cold water.

Couscous with Sicilian Flavours

This couscous has Sicilian flavours: ginger, tomatoes, garlic and vegetables. With North Africa a few short miles from the island of Sicily, it is no surprise that couscous is one of the island specialities (though traditionally it is prepared with fish).

I like this as a side dish with Pan-Grilled Mediterranean Vegetables (*see Chapter 6, page 136*) or Verdure Arrosti (*see Chapter 6, page 134*).

SERVES 4 AS A SIDE DISH

3 cloves	garlic, chopped
2 tbsp	extra virgin olive oil
200 g/7 oz/1 cup	diced tomatoes (tinned is fine; if using fresh, sauté them first over a high heat to intensify their flavours)
250 g/8 oz	green beans, topped and tailed and cut into bite-sized pieces
500 ml/16 fl oz/2 cups	vegetable stock (or water mixed with a stock cube), more if needed
375 g/12 oz/2¼ cups	instant couscous
½ tsp	powdered ginger, or to taste
dash	of Tabasco or pinch of cayenne pepper
	salt to taste

1) Lightly sauté the garlic in the olive oil then add the tomatoes and beans and cook together for about 5 minutes over a high heat. Add the stock, reduce the heat, and cook for another 5 minutes.
2) Stir in the couscous, remove from the heat, cover and leave for a further 5 minutes, then lift the lid to check on the moistness of the couscous. If it seems a bit dry, add a little more stock. Return the lid and leave to sit for a few more moments.
3) Fork in the ginger, Tabasco or cayenne and salt, then return to the heat to warm through completely for a few moments. Serve right away.

Piatti di Verdure
Vegetable Main Dishes

Vegetables – whether boiled or simmered, grilled or barbecued, roasted, baked or sautéed – are doted on at the Italian table. Many are dishes that might not traditionally be eaten as a main course, or have been adapted for vegetarians. Following are several of my favourites, all of which can be varied as desired to accommodate the season and your tastes.

Verdure Arrosti

Peppers, aubergines (eggplants), courgettes (zucchini), tomatoes, fennel and onions, all brushed with olive oil and roasted or grilled, make a quintessential Mediterranean vegetable feast. Make a double or even triple portion, and dice the leftovers for next-day salads, pastas and sandwiches, or to toss together for a roasted-vegetable ratatouille.

SERVES 4

1 aubergine (eggplant), sliced into quarters or thick slices

2 courgettes (zucchini), cut lengthways

1 red, 1 yellow and 1 green peppers

1 red onion, cut into halves lengthways

1 fennel, halved or quartered

4 ripe tomatoes, halved

extra virgin olive oil, to taste

salt and freshly ground black pepper, to taste

balsamic or red wine vinegar, as desired

pinch of whichever herbs you desire: dried oregano, fresh basil or marjoram, chopped parsley

1) Arrange the vegetables on a baking sheet or in a shallow baking dish. Brush generously with olive oil and sprinkle with salt and pepper.
2) Grill the vegetables until slightly browned in spots and just tender inside. Turn them several times until they reach this state and are cooked through evenly.
3) Serve on a platter, with a cruet of olive oil, one of balsamic or red wine vinegar, and sprinkle the vegetables with the herbs of choice.

Pan-Grilled Mediterranean Vegetables

It is amazing that a simple preparation – grilling the vegetables and lavishing them with olive oil, garlic and fresh basil – can produce such delicious results. Using already-roasted red peppers is pricey, but saves time.

SERVES 4

4	small to medium courgettes (zucchini), cut lengthways into very thin slices
1	small to medium aubergine (eggplant), cut lengthways into very thin slices
4	small ripe tomatoes, cut into halves crossways
1	raw sliced bulb of fennel or 2 blanched whole artichoke hearts, sliced (optional)
	salt to taste
1 small jar	roasted red peppers (or 4 red peppers, roasted and peeled; I do this the day before)
About 30 g/1 oz/1 cup	fresh, sweet basil
1–2 cloves	garlic, finely chopped
2–3 tbsp,	or more as desired, extra virgin olive oil
a few drops	either lemon juice or balsamic vinegar
	coarsely ground pepper, to taste

1) Sprinkle the courgettes (zucchini), aubergine (eggplant), tomatoes and fennel or artichokes if using, with salt and set aside.
2) Lightly spread or rub a heavy grill pan or frying pan with olive oil and heat it until just smoking.
3) Place the courgettes (zucchini) and aubergine (eggplant) in small batches on the grill pan or frying pan to quickly brown on each side, then remove them to a plate. Repeat with the tomatoes, fennel and/or artichokes hearts, and finally warm the peppers.
4) Serve sprinkled with the basil, garlic, olive oil and lemon juice or balsamic vinegar and seasoned with the black pepper.

Vegetable Stew with Olive Oil and Lemon

Along the Amalfi coast, lemons grow in lush profusion and are eaten in risotti, soups, salads and even stews, such as the following one that livens up winter's hearty vegetables.

SERVES 4

2	onions, cut into chunks
3–5 cloves	garlic, cut into chunks or slices
4	medium to large carrots, cut into bite-sized chunks
8	boiling potatoes, peeled and halved
500 ml/16 fl oz/2 cups	vegetable stock (or water mixed with a vegetable stock cube)
1	medium cabbage, cut into bite-sized pieces or strips
250–350 g/8–12 oz	green runner beans, cut into bite-sized pieces
	coarse black pepper, to taste
2–3 tbsp	chopped parsley (preferably flat-leaf Italian parsley)
	extra virgin olive oil, as desired
2	lemons, cut into wedges

1) In a heavy saucepan place the onions, garlic, carrots and potatoes with the stock. Bring to the boil, then reduce the heat and cook until the vegetables are almost tender but still slightly crunchy (about 15 minutes). Add the cabbage and runner beans and cook, covered, for another 10 minutes. Season with coarse black pepper to taste.

2) Serve sprinkled with parsley, and accompany with a cruet of olive oil and wedges of lemon for squeezing on as desired.

Melanzane con Ricotta

Rich, meaty aubergine (eggplant) topped with snowy, fresh ricotta, and the vivacious flavours of garlic and fresh tomatoes, makes this simply prepared dish one of my favourite summer meals.

Serve with any tomatoey, lively pasta dish.

SERVES 4

1	medium-large aubergine (eggplant), sliced thinly
3 tbsp	extra virgin olive oil, or as needed
175 g/6 oz	ricotta cheese
5 cloves	garlic, chopped
5	ripe tomatoes, thinly sliced
	(tinned will not do here)
4–6 tbsp	freshly grated Parmesan cheese or pecorino
several handfuls	of fresh basil, thinly sliced

1) Heat the grill.
2) Arrange the aubergine (eggplant) slices on a baking sheet and brush with olive oil. Grill first on one side then the other until both sides are lightly browned in spots and the aubergine (eggplant) is just tender.
3) Top each slice of aubergine (eggplant) with a thin layer of ricotta, a sprinkling of garlic, a slice or two of tomato, then more garlic and a generous sprinkling of Parmesan or pecorino.
4) Drizzle the remaining olive oil over the top then place under the grill and cook until the cheese turns lightly golden brown.
5) Serve right away, with the fresh basil sprinkled over the top.

Winter Squash (Pumpkin) with Beans and Greens

This tastes super, and is as healthy as it is yummy: pumpkin, beans and greens, with tomatoes and olive oil. A little Parmesan might be a bit rich, but it adds such seductive flavour. Serve as a main plate with bread for scooping up the vegetables with. You might begin the meal with a light little soup such as Broccoli Soup (*see Chapter 3, page 46*).

SERVES 4

1	smallish winter squash such as acorn squash, hubbard squash, pumpkin, etc. – 1 kg/2¼ lb in total, about 450 g/1 lb when peeled and seeded
1	small to medium onion, thinly sliced or coarsely chopped
3 tbsp	extra virgin olive oil
3 cloves	garlic, thinly sliced or slivered
8 ripe	smallish fresh tomatoes, diced or cut into smallish chunks
pinch	of sugar
	salt and freshly ground black pepper to taste
400 g/14 oz	cooked, drained borlotti beans (tinned is fine)
¼ tsp	dried sage leaves, crumbled, or several fresh sage leaves, chopped
1 bunch	chard (silver beets) or spinach leaves, cut into thin slices or strips crossways
	freshly grated Parmesan cheese, as desired

1) Peel the squash and slice it about ½-inch thick, and into bite-sized lengths. Lightly sauté the onion in the olive oil until softened, then add the garlic and the squash and cook for about 5 minutes, turning once or twice and taking care not to break up the squash but to let it brown lightly.

2) Add the tomatoes, sugar, salt and pepper, and cook over a medium-high heat until the tomatoes form a sauce-like mixture, then stir in the beans and sage, and finally the chard or spinach and cook, turning once or twice, until the greens heat through, wilt and are bright green and tender.

3) Sprinkle generously with the Parmesan, and serve.

Asparagus and Eggs with Truffle Oil

You can use one or two eggs: one egg makes a good starter, while two eggs make a good main dish. You might like to follow this with Pan-Grilled Mediterranean Vegetables (*see Chapter 6, page 136*), or start with Tomato Broth with Peas and Little Pastas (*see Chapter 3, page 40*).

This is a rich and luxurious dish, one that can only get richer and more luxurious with additions: a truffle shaved over the top is bliss, so too is a handful of sautéed diced porcini. Be sure to use excellent quality Parmesan.

When using truffle oil, you only need a few drops to impart a heady aroma. Some brands of truffle oil retain their aroma better than others. Be sure to keep the lid sealed tightly and the little bottle out of the reach of either strong light or heat. I store mine in the refrigerator if it is for longer than a week or two once opened, though it solidifies and needs to warm to room temperature if it is to drip out of the bottle.

SERVES 4

1 bunch	asparagus, tough ends trimmed
5–6 cloves	garlic, or as desired, coarsely chopped
4–6 tbsp	butter
4	eggs as a starter, 8 eggs as a main course, preferably free-range
90 g/3 oz/1½ cups	or as desired Parmesan cheese, thinly shaved or freshly grated
a few drops	of truffle oil

1) Steam or boil the asparagus until *al dente*, then remove from the heat.
2) Meanwhile, heat the garlic with the butter until the butter melts and smells fabulous; do not let it brown or fry. Pour off and reserve about half the garlic butter, leaving just enough behind to cook the eggs in.
3) Gently crack open each egg into a saucer or bowl, then slip it into the hot butter, over a medium-low heat. When all of the eggs are in the pan, spoon a little of the garlic butter over the top, then cover and cook over a low heat for 2–3 minutes or until the whites are firm and the yolks still quite runny but covered with a thin veil. If the pan is big enough, arrange the asparagus around the eggs to warm with them, otherwise, warm them separately.
4) Serve right away, the warmed asparagus and eggs sprinkled with a few drops of the truffle oil, then blanketed with freshly grated or thinly shaved Parmesan.

Brown Lentils in Spicy Tomato Sauce

Serve this warming lentil stew ladled into soup bowls, or spooned over crisp bruschetta as a first course. Leftovers are nice served atop a simple white wine risotto, and also make a good basis for a hefty minestrone.

SERVES 4

175 g/6 oz/1 cup	green/brown lentils or lentils de Puy (French, firm, similar to a type of regional Italian lentils and delicious in this recipe)
3	bay leaves
1	onion, chopped
5 cloves	garlic, sliced
½	hot red chilli pepper, or ½ tsp mild chilli powder, or to taste
300 g/12 oz/1¾ cups	diced tomatoes (tinned is fine)
a few drops	of vinegar
	salt and freshly ground black pepper
several sprigs	of fresh marjoram, coarsely chopped

1) In a covered saucepan, cook the lentils with the bay leaves in enough water to cover by about 2 inches. They should be just tender in about 20 minutes.
2) Meanwhile, sauté the onion, garlic and chilli pepper until the onions are just soft, then stir in the tomatoes and cook down until thickened, about 15 minutes.
3) Drain the lentils, saving the liquid in case you need it to thin down the stew or use as the basis for a soup. Combine the lentils and tomato mixture, add a few drops of vinegar, salt and pepper to taste and marjoram. Heat together, adding some of the cooking liquid if needed to keep it the consistency of a thick stew or porridge, but not so thick as to burn.
4) Serve warm.

Contorni/Vegetable Side Dishes

When I'm in Italy, I sometimes feast on *contorni* – those little vegetables dishes that are eaten on the side – instead of ordering a main course. Many *contorni* can also be enjoyed as an *antipasto*.

Patate con Basilica

Fragrant with sweet basil, this dish consists of creamy mashed potatoes green with pesto. You can use commercial good-quality pesto if you like; but if you are awash in fresh basil, use that instead.

This recipe is good with almost anything pan-browned or barbecued. I like it with vegetarian sausages, and an *antipasto* of Spinaci (o Verdure) con Mozzarella (*see Chapter 1, page 12*).

SERVES 4

6	large baking potatoes, peeled and cut into quarters or bite-sized chunks
4–6 cloves	garlic, chopped
3 tbsp	butter
2 tbsp	cream, milk, or crème fraîche (Italian creams are often slightly soured)
3–5 tbsp	pesto or finely chopped basil mixed with a tbsp or two of olive oil and grated Parmesan)
	salt and freshly ground black pepper to taste

1) Place the potatoes in a saucepan with water to cover and half the garlic. Bring to the boil and cook until the potatoes are tender, about 15 minutes.
2) Remove from the heat and drain, reserving the garlic-scented potato broth for next-day soup.
3) Mash the potatoes and season with the reserved raw garlic, the butter, cream or milk, pesto and salt and pepper. Serve immediately.

Grilled Pesto Asparagus

Tossing asparagus with pesto brings out the sweet grassy flavour of the asparagus, and the olive oil keeps it all moist and succulent. Grilling keeps the asparagus crunchy and crisp, and makes a luscious dish to eat as an *antipasto* or as a main dish, topped with shavings of Parmesan and surrounded by garlic-rubbed toasts spread with goat's cheese or olivada (black olive paste).

Serve alongside a big tomatoey pasta dish, such as Hot Pasta with a Cool Sauce (*see Chapter 4, page 58*) or Macaroni con Pomadori (*see Chapter 4, page 66*).

SERVES 4

1	large bunch asparagus, preferably medium-sized green asparagus (about 450 g/1 lb), trimmed of their tough ends (save for soups, etc.)
3 cloves	garlic, chopped
2 tbsp	pesto
3 tbsp	extra virgin olive oil
juice of ½	lemon

1) Combine the asparagus with the garlic, pesto, olive oil and lemon juice. Leave for 5 or 10 minutes if you have the time.
2) Arrange the asparagus on a baking sheet and place under a hot grill. Cook for about 5 minutes on each side or until lightly browned and crisp.

Broccoli with Garlic and Olive Oil

Broccoli, cooked until just tender then sautéed quickly with olive oil and garlic, is the quintessential flavour of Tuscany, though a shake of hot pepper flakes gives it the lusty taste of the sun-drenched south. Choose according to your desires.

Other greens, such as broccoli de rape or rabe, or kale, can be used in place of the broccoli. Besides a side dish, this also makes a terrific *antipasto*, and is good sandwiched between two halves of a crusty roll alongside a slab of fresh mozzarella, for a mid-afternoon *panino*.

SERVES 4

1	large or 2 small-to-medium heads of broccoli, cut into bite-sized pieces, the stem peeled and cut into bite-sized pieces
2–3 tbsp	extra virgin olive oil
3 cloves	garlic, chopped
	salt and coarsely ground black pepper or red pepper flakes, to taste
juice of ½	lemon, or to taste

1) Steam or boil the broccoli until bright green and crisp-tender (only about 3 minutes or so). Drain and rinse in cold water to cool.

2) Meanwhile, combine the oil and garlic in a frying pan and warm until fragrant, then add the broccoli, salt, and pepper or red pepper flakes. Stir and cook for 5 minutes or so, then add the lemon juice and cook a minute or so longer. Do not let the broccoli cook to a grey colour; it should be tender but still green.

3) Serve hot or let it cool to room temperature.

Winter Squash with Garlic

Eat this as a spread for crostini or bruschetta, or as a sauce for grilled or poached foods. Serve it as an *antipasto*, as well, especially to begin a meal of richer, heavier dishes.

SERVES 4

1	small to medium orange-coloured winter squash or pumpkin – about 1 kg/2¼ lb
1–2 cloves	garlic, chopped
1–2 tbsp	extra virgin olive oil
	salt and freshly ground black pepper, to taste
juice of ¼–½	lemon, or to taste
several tbsp	fresh basil, thinly sliced, or ¼ tsp dried herbs de Provence, or ¼ tsp dried basil, crumbled

1) Cut the squash into halves and remove the seeds with a spoon (save the seeds to toast in the oven, seasoned with a little soy sauce and salt, for a crunchy snack). Cut the squash halves into several chunks each, then place in a steamer or a saucepan with water to cover. Bring to the boil, and cook over a high heat, covered, until the squash is just tender (10–15 minutes). If boiling, season the water with a pinch of sugar and salt.

2) When the squash is tender, remove from the heat.

3) Take the squash from the pan and, using a spoon, scrape away the flesh and discard the skin. Mash the flesh with the chopped garlic, then work in the olive oil, salt and pepper, and lemon juice. Taste for seasoning and serve at room temperature, sprinkled with basil or *herbs de Provence*.

Pan-Roasted Fennel

Leftover fennel is delicious diced and tossed into a simple next-day tomato sauce for pasta. Serve it as a side dish or as an *antipasto* mixed with shiny black oil-cured olives.

SERVES 4

4–6	small-to-medium bulbs fennel, cut into quarters or halves
3 tbsp	olive oil
1	onion, chopped
4 cloves	garlic, chopped
¼ tsp	fennel seeds
	salt and freshly ground black pepper, plus a pinch of sugar if needed
⅛ tsp or to taste	oregano leaves, crumbled
125 ml/4 fl oz/½ cup	vegetable stock (or water mixed with ¼–½ vegetable stock cube)
juice of ¼–½	lemon, or to taste

1) Sauté the fennel in a heavy frying pan with the olive oil, onion, garlic, fennel seeds, salt, pepper, sugar and oregano. Add the stock, then cover tightly and place on top of the stove and cook over a very low heat until tender; this should take about 20 minutes.

2) Heat the grill, then place the frying pan under the grill and cook the fennel mixture to crisp up the top. Serve it with a squeeze of lemon.

3) Let the roasted fennel cool to room temperature, then cut it into dice.

4) Enjoy warm or leave it to cool to room temperature.

Porcini Mushrooms Roasted in Foil

Roasting foods quickly in individual packages seals in the flavour, and is exquisitely simple to do. Plus there is no washing up of pans.

Practicality aside, it is a superbly sensual way to enjoy a food – when the parcel arrives on your plate and is opened, the strong scent of your foresty mushrooms is released in a deliciously odorous steam.

A selection of porcini and their stems are fine; be sure the stems are chopped into small pieces. If porcini are too expensive, use a combination of any mushrooms you like, even the common cultivated ones. For optimum flavour, include at least a small amount of porcini.

Though you can easily cook them in the oven, they are also great as a starter when you are having a barbecue – just toss the foil parcels onto the coals and leave for 5 or 10 minutes, then remove and serve.

SERVES 4

4	large squares of foil
6 tbsp	extra virgin olive oil, or as desired
About 250 g/8 oz/8⅓ cups	porcini mushrooms, cut into bite-sized pieces
4 or more cloves	garlic, chopped
2 tbsp	chopped flat-leaf parsley
pinch	of fresh thyme or finely chopped mint
	salt, a fine grating of nutmeg (if using thyme rather than mint), a pinch of black pepper, to taste

1) Preheat the oven to 200°C/400°F/gas mark 6.
2) Brush each square of foil with olive oil, then divide the mushrooms between the squares. Sprinkle with garlic, parsley, thyme or mint, salt, nutmeg (if using) and pepper, then drizzle with the rest of the oil.
3) Bring the corners of each square of foil up to meet in the centre, and fold over to seal tightly.
4) Bake the mushrooms for 10–15 minutes, depending on their size and age. Serve the mushrooms in their foil and let each diner open his or her parcel. Accompany with crusty bread to soak up the tasty juices.

Casseroles and Stews

Though casseroles and stews are traditionally long-cooked affairs, the following vegetarian ones cook just long enough to become tender and, if topped with cheese, to get a crusty, melting topping.

Mazzamurru

With flavours much like a pizza, the traditional Sardinian mazzamurru, or baked casserole of bread, tomatoes and cheese, is hefty and filling for the coldest of nights, yet it is easy to toss together. You need no more than a crisp little salad of mixed greens as a fresh counterpoint for this lusty meal. It's also a great way to use up leftover bread.

SERVES 4

175 g/6 oz/³/₄ cup	tomato purée
1 kg/2¹/₄ lb/6 cups	ripe tomatoes, diced or 2 tins diced tomatoes packed in juice (include the juices)
3–5 cloves	garlic, chopped
handful	of whole fresh basil leaves
450 g/1 lb	stale country bread, cut into slices
250–350 g/8–12 oz/1¹/₂–2 cups	mild white cheese such as mozzarella, thinly sliced
125 g/4 oz/2 cups	grated Parmesan or pecorino cheese, shredded
250 g/8 fl oz/³/₄ cup	vegetable stock
60 ml/2 fl oz/¹/₄ cup	extra virgin olive oil

1) In the bottom of a casserole smear a few tbsp of the tomato purée then layer with some of the tomatoes. Sprinkle with a little garlic and basil then layer the bread and cheeses, and keep repeating, ending with a cheese layer.
2) Pour the stock over the top, drizzle with the olive oil and bake at 190°C/375°F/gas mark 5 for 25 minutes or until crusty on top with the bread soft, yet not too soupy. Serve right away.

Polenta al Forno

Polenta – layered with tomatoes, cheese and fresh rosemary – then baked until sizzling is warming and delicious. It is at its easiest when the polenta is prepared a day ahead and is then firm and easy to layer. You could also use ready-made polenta, cooked up and sold in rolls ready to be cut and layered with sauce and cheese.

While the polenta is baking, you could throw together an *antipasto* or two: Sweet-sour *Antipasto* of Beetroot (*see Chapter 1, page 10*), a plate of olives, and perhaps a handful of blanched green beans tossed with a little olive oil, white wine vinegar and a sprinkling of fresh basil.

SERVES 4

200 g/7 oz	polenta (instant cooking), cut into thick slices
	water as directed on packet
400 g/14 oz/2⅓ cups	diced tomatoes (tinned is fine, use the ones packed in juice)
3 cloves	garlic, chopped
2–3 tbsp	fresh rosemary, chopped
250 g/8 oz/1½ cups	mozzarella, fontina or any mild white cheese such as Edam, thinly sliced
110–125 g/3–4 oz/1¾–2 cups	Parmesan, grated or shredded
3 tbsp	olive oil

1) Cook the polenta according to the packet directions; quick-cooking polenta takes only 5 minutes.
2) Pour it onto an oiled and/or non-stick baking sheet and place in the refrigerator to cool for about 10 minutes.
3) When the polenta is firm enough to slice, layer some of the diced tomatoes on the bottom of a casserole, then sprinkle with garlic, rosemary, polenta, cheese and olive oil, ending with a layer of tomatoes, cheese and olive oil.
4) Bake at 200°C/400°F/gas mark 6 for about 15 minutes or long enough for the dish to heat through and the cheese to melt.

Three Bean and Porcini Stew

Though porcini are fragrant and delicious used by themselves in this delicious rustic dish, if you have a selection of several different types, use as many as you like. Ditto for the beans – if you have red kidney beans, add them, but don't add black beans as it turns the dish into a greyish sludge (though delicious). Although canned beans are never preferable to long-simmered dried beans, they are quick and convenient, and very nice when oomphed up with lots of other flavours such as here.

An *antipasti* selection is probably a good way to begin this hearty, wintery meal, along with crusty bread or ciabatta for soaking up the rich mushroomy juices.

SERVES 4

5–8	shallots, chopped
3–4 tbsp	olive oil
1 clove	garlic, thinly sliced
500 ml/16 fl oz/2 cups	vegetable stock of choice (a soup cube mixed with water is fine)
125 ml/4 fl oz/½ cup	dry white wine
handful (about 1–2 tbsp) each:	porcini, morels or mousserons, chanterelles, etc., broken into small pieces
1 tin (400 g/14 oz each):	borlotti beans, cannellini beans and butter beans, drained
	salt and freshly ground black pepper, to taste

1) Lightly sauté the shallots in the olive oil until soft (about 5 minutes), then stir in the garlic, vegetable stock, wine and mushrooms. Bring to boil, then reduce the heat, add the beans and seasoning.
2) Simmer for about 10 minutes or until the liquid is flavourful. If the liquid is too thin, boil over a high heat for another 5–10 minutes or until it thickens.
3) Serve with crusty bread or steamed rice.

Bruschetta, Crostini, Frittate, Panini (Sandwiches), Pizze (Pizzas) and Pastries

Little savoury things on bread are one of the pleasures of a nibble with a glass of wine, or as a starter for nearly any supper. Whether bruschetta, crostini, panini or pizza, you basically have a zesty spread on top of bread or bread dough.

A Frittata makes an excellent sandwich filling, too, one you'll find in many guises in Italy's *caffe-bars*, alongside savoury pastries such as the cheese-and-pesto filled Basil and Pepper Calzone (*see page 173*).

Bean Bruschetta with Arugula (Rocket)

Bruschetta (pronounced bru-sketta) is simply bread toasted (at its best over an open fire or barbecue) then rubbed with garlic, and drizzled with the best olive oil you can find. When made with the freshly crushed olives of the season, this humble dish is one of the finest on earth.

Bruschetta is the original garlic bread, in its austere form, no more than essence of garlic, bread and olive oil. But this basic food is doted on and eaten with a myriad of embellishments. One of the best is simply to top it with ripe sliced tomatoes and basil – a Tuscan summer favourite. Another is the following dish of puréed beans and rocket leaves piled on top of the bruschetta.

Any tender simmered beans can be ladled over bruschetta: borlotti are very good, too, especially fresh ones (cranberry beans or cocos). And if you don't have arugula (rocket), use any wild flavourful greens you can find.

This starter is great after-work everyday fare, and equally good for sharing with friends. Follow with a pasta that is full of light, lively flavours and lots of fresh vegetables, such as Penne con Asparagi (*see Chapter 4, page 69*).

SERVES 4

2 cups	cooked cannellini beans
8 small or 4 large slices	baguette, cut diagonally
4–6 cloves	garlic, halved
3–5 tbsp	olive oil
60–90 g/2–3 oz/1–1½ cups	or so Parmesan cheese, shaved with a vegetable peeler
	handful of arugula (rocket)

1) Warm the beans in their liquid. Meanwhile, toast the baguette on each side until golden, then rub each side with the garlic and drizzle lightly with the olive oil.

2) Place these garlicky toasts on plates and spoon the drained, cooked beans over them, then sprinkle with the shaved Parmesan and leaves of the arugula (rocket).

3) Serve right away.

Artichoke and Cheese Crostini

Crostini are crisp toasts topped with a variety of savoury mixtures – more or less anything you want. Often crostini are thin slices of bread – baguettes are great because they are thin, flute-like loaves – and fried until crisp. I prefer to brush them lightly with olive oil and toast them, then spread them with my choice of topping.

Serve as a starter or as party fare, or for an afternoon nibble.

SERVES 4

1	baguette, country loaf, pain levain or ciabatta, thinly sliced diagonally
1–2 cloves	garlic, chopped
1 85-g/3-oz jar	artichoke paste
125 g/4 oz	feta cheese, thinly sliced
175 g/6 oz/1 cup	mild melting cheese, such as mozzarella, shredded
a drizzle	olive oil

1) Lightly toast the bread in a hot oven on both sides until crisp, then remove from the oven and rub or toss with the chopped garlic.
2) Spread the artichoke paste over the bread and layer first the feta then the mild melting cheese and a drizzle of olive oil. Grill until the cheese melts and lightly bubbles in places. Serve right away.

Tosta alla Milanese

Tostas are Milanese toasted cheese sandwiches, sold from *caffe-bars* throughout the city, with a selection of assorted condiments arranged on the bar for customers to help themselves to, spooning them into the melted cheese sandwich. Besides giardiniera, that tangy mixture of pickled vegetables, you might find capers, roasted red peppers, mustard, chopped herbs, onion, and so forth. I put a little chopped garlic in my sandwiches, but the Milanese I have met find this crude (I find it delicious).

SERVES 4

8 slices	country bread
175–250 g/6–8 oz/1–1½ cups	fontina or other mild meltable white cheese, coarsely shredded
a little	chopped fresh garlic (optional)
	roasted red peppers from a jar, about 2 peppers in total or 4–6 tbsp if measuring them in strips
several leaves	of basil, thinly sliced
3–4 tbsp	softened butter or olive oil

1) Lay 4 slices of bread on a surface and arrange half of the cheese on it, then top with the garlic, peppers and basil, then the rest of the cheese. Top with the second set of bread slices and press down well.

2) Melt the butter or heat the olive oil in a frying pan and brown the sandwiches on both sides (use a sandwich toaster if you have one). Placing a heavy weight on top of the browning sandwich helps get a good crisp brown colour and firm quality to the sandwich.

Variations

Substitute giardiniera for the roasted red peppers; use mustard spread on the bread instead of the basil.

Roasted Pepper and Fresh Pecorino Frittata

Frittate are flat, thick omelettes, filled with vegetables and cooked until firm. They are great peasant fare but doted on in the city as well. A frittata might be eaten hot for an informal, satisfying supper, or left to cool and eaten in wedges as part of the *antipasto*. Frittate also make a fine sandwich filling, stuffed between the covers of a plump roll or foccacio.

Any vegetables – cooked spinach, peas, sautéed mushrooms, diced lightly browned potatoes, shredded or diced courgettes (zucchini), ripe sliced tomatoes – are all excellent frittate fillers. And leftover pasta or spaghetti make a good addition too, and a great way of using up what otherwise might go to waste. Combine the pasta with the beaten egg, a bit of grated cheese, and pour it into the hot olive-oiled pan.

Roasted pepper and tangy fresh cheese is delicious cooked in the cloak of egg that makes up a frittata. If you do not have fresh pecorino, use feta, or even Indian paneer, though with paneer you will need to add a bit of extra salt, and perhaps a generous grating of fresh Parmesan.

Serve for supper: start with a little Broad (Fava) Bean Soup with Tiny Pastas (*see Chapter 3, page 36*) and accompany the frittata with tiny boiled potatoes dressed with olive oil and sliced spring onions.

SERVES 4

1 each:	roasted, peeled and sliced red and green pepper or one jar roasted red peppers, well drained and rinsed
3 cloves	garlic, chopped
3 tbsp	extra virgin olive oil
4	eggs, lightly beaten
125–175 g/4–6 oz	fresh pecorino cheese or feta cheese, diced
	salt and freshly ground black pepper
	dried oregano, crumbled, to taste

1) Lightly sauté the peppers with the garlic in half the olive oil for only a minute or two, to warm through and bring out their flavours. Remove from the pan and stir into the beaten eggs along with the cheese, taking care not to break up the cheese too much.

2) Heat the remaining oil in the pan and pour in the egg-pepper mixture. Cook over a medium heat until the bottom is golden brown then place it under the grill and cook the top. Sprinkle with the salt, pepper and oregano and serve right away.

Courgette (Zucchini) Frittata

When courgette (zucchini) flowers – delicate and golden – are available, I might slice up a handful and include them in the following frittata, adding them just before the eggs.

As a supper dish, serve a plate of ripe sliced tomatoes garnished with basil and glistening black olives alongside, all drizzled with olive oil and balsamic vinegar.

SERVES 2

4	small to medium courgettes (zucchini), diced
2–3 tbsp	olive oil
2 cloves	garlic, chopped
	salt and freshly ground black pepper, to taste
125 g/4 oz/¾ cup	fontina or mozzarella cheese, or other nicely melting cheese, diced
4	eggs, lightly beaten
1–2 tbsp	milk, or as desired
2 tbsp	fresh basil, finely chopped or thinly sliced
4–6 tbsp	freshly grated Parmesan cheese, to sprinkle over the top

1) Lightly sauté the courgettes (zucchini) in half the olive oil until lightly browned in spots and just tender. Stir in the garlic, season with salt and pepper, then pour into a bowl.

2) Meanwhile, combine the cheese with the eggs, milk and basil, then stir in the cooked courgettes (zucchini).

3) Heat the rest of the oil in the frying pan, then pour in the courgette (zucchini)-egg mixture and cook over a medium-low heat until the bottom turns golden.

4) Grill until the top cooks and turns lightly browned in spots and the fritatta is no longer runny.

5) Sprinkle generously with Parmesan which will melt a little with the heat, and serve either hot, warm or cool.

Tortino di Pomodori

Like most frittate, this tomato frittata is good warm but even better cold, especially eaten on a piece of bread as part of an *antipasto* for a late-summer supper.

SERVES 4

1	onion, chopped
3 cloves	garlic, chopped
3 tbsp	extra virgin olive oil
6–8	ripe tomatoes, coarsely chopped or diced
¼	red pepper, chopped
	salt and freshly ground black pepper, to taste
pinch	of sugar, to taste
6	eggs, lightly beaten
2–3 tsp	fresh marjoram or oregano, coarsely chopped
175 g/6 oz/1 cup	mozzarella or feta cheese, sliced
4–6 tbsp	freshly grated Parmesan cheese
2 tbsp	fresh basil leaves, torn or coarsely chopped

1) Lightly sauté the onion and garlic in the olive oil until softened, then add the tomatoes and red pepper, salt, pepper and sugar to taste. Cook over a medium-low heat, stirring every so often, until the tomatoes are sauce-like (about 10 minutes).
2) Pour in the eggs without stirring, then add the marjoram or oregano and cook until the bottom of the eggs are golden and firm but the top is still wet and custardy.
3) Add the cheese, swirl to let some of the soft egg cover it, then blanket the top with the Parmesan.
4) Cook under the grill until the egg mixture feels firmed and the cheese is melted and lightly golden in places.
5) Sprinkle with basil or more marjoram or oregano, and eat hot or leave to cool.

Basil and Pepper Calzone

These crisp cheese-and-pesto-filled pastries are pure street-food pleasure, quickly rolled out, stuffed and baked to accompany glasses of cooling wine on a summer's evening or a treat for any picnic, though I do like them best when hot.

SERVES 4

500 g/16 oz	puff pastry
4 tbsp	pesto
250–300 g/8–10 oz/ 1½–1¾ cups	mozzarella or fontina cheese, diced
1	roasted red pepper, cut into strips or bite-sized pieces, or about 3 tbsp if taken from a jar
1	large ripe tomato, diced or 2 tbsp tinned diced tomatoes, drained
175 g/6 oz	ricotta cheese
1 clove	garlic, chopped

1) Divide the pastry into 4 pieces and roll into round, flat discs. Place on a baking sheet.
2) Spread half of each pastry with the pesto, taking care to leave a space around the edge for sealing.
3) Mix the remaining ingredients and place a spoonful or so on top of the pesto-spread dough. You'll probably have some leftover cheese mixture – this is delicious on tomorrow night's crostini or pasta.
4) Fold the pastry over, wetting the edges with a little water, then press to seal.

5) Bake at 200°C/400°F/gas mark 6 for 15–20 minutes or until golden brown. Eat very hot, the cheese dripping in sizzling little strings.

Piadine e Pizze/Topped Piadinas and Pizzas

Following is a selection of bread-based snacks topped with vegetables, olives, aromatics and cheeses.

Piadine, available occasionally in Italian delis in Britain, are flat wheat-flour pancakes from northern Italy, near Bologna, where they are served with various savoury toppings: most often cheese, salumerie (salami, cooked meats etc.) or vegetables. The piadina is very similar to flour tortillas, the Mexican pancake-like flatbread easily available in supermarkets, so I usually use tortillas.

Pizzas are so universally enjoyed that it might be hard to remember that when they originated in Naples they were little more than pieces of dough topped with a smear of tomato and baked. The toppings came later, and they are still coming. First the various regions of Italy, then the neighbouring areas, then out into the world. Traditional pizza toppings are hard to beat, however.

Since preparing dough takes longer than a 30-minute cook has time for, using focaccio, flour tortillas, thick country bread such as pain levain or baguette and good-quality pizza bases can all make a very fine 'pizza', if slightly veered off the path from the original.

Pizza al' Asparagi

If you can't find good pizza bases, make your own dough and keep it in the refrigerator, ready to be defrosted at a moment's notice in the microwave. Or use focaccio.

When asparagus is in season, it makes one of my favourite pizza toppings. I first tasted asparagus pizza in Florence, a wedge bought and eaten while walking in the summer rain.

SERVES 4	
1 bunch	asparagus, cut into bite-sized pieces, tough ends trimmed
3–4 tbsp	tomato purée
4	individual pizza bases (good-quality ones)
or 4	portions of good focaccio
3–4	ripe tomatoes, diced (tinned diced tomatoes are acceptable, but fresh are preferable)
small pinch	of sugar
	salt and freshly ground black pepper
3 cloves	garlic, chopped
3 tbsp	thinly sliced basil
175–250 g/6–8 oz/1–1½ cups	shredded white cheese such as fontina or mozzarella
3–4 tbsp	extra virgin olive oil
	freshly grated Parmesan cheese, as desired

1) Preheat the oven to 190°C/375°F/gas mark 5.
2) Lightly cook the asparagus by either boiling or steaming. Cook only until brighter in colour but still too crunchy to eat. Remove from heat and drain well.
3) Spread the tomato purée onto the pizza bases or foccacio, then top with the tomatoes, a pinch of sugar, salt and pepper, the reserved asparagus, garlic, basil, fontina or mozzarella, a drizzling of the olive oil and a good shake of the Parmesan.
4) Bake for 15–20 minutes or just long enough to melt the cheese to a crispy, bubbling topping. Serve right away.

Thin Pesto 'Pizza' with Herb Salad

If you can, cook this over a barbecue, taking care to keep the pizzas at the cooler end of the heat, or on top of a piece of foil if the grill is close to the flame. And do cover it: let the smoke permeate the pizza and also melt the cheese.

The herb salad of chopped parsley and arugula (rocket), sprinkled on top at the end, enhance the other flavours deliciously and freshly, rather than calling attention to themselves. The olive oil is an important part of the pizza: it somehow unifies the rest of the ingredients.

SERVES 4

4	flour tortillas, the larger the better
2–3 cloves	garlic, chopped
4–5	ripe tomatoes (or tinned), diced
4–5 tbsp	pesto, or as desired
175–250 g/6–8 oz/1–1½ cups	mild white cheese such as mozzarella, Monterey Jack or any British Cheddar, shredded
1–2 tbsp	olive oil
2 tbsp each:	chopped parsley and chopped arugula leaves (roquette, rocket)

1) Top the tortillas first with a sprinkling of garlic, then the tomatoes, dollops of the pesto and a layer of the cheese. Drizzle the top with olive oil, then carefully place each 'pizza' on top of the barbecue grill, or on top of a piece of foil on the barbecue (*see introduction, above*), or under the grill.

2) Barbecue, covered, or grill until the cheese melts. Take care when you retrieve the pizza from the barbecue that the topping doesn't slide off and onto the coals.

3) Serve the pizza right away, each sprinkled with the chopped parsley and arugula (rocket).

Artichoke Heart and Goat's Cheese Pizza

SERVES 4

4	purchased pizza bases
4–6 oz	goat's cheese of choice
3–4 cloves	garlic, finely chopped
½ tsp	thyme leaves, crumbled
1 jar	marinated artichokes, drained
125–175 g/4–6 oz/¾–1 cup	shredded mozzarella cheese
4–6 tbsp	freshly grated Parmesan cheese
1–2 tbsp	extra virgin olive oil for drizzling, or as desired

1) Arrange the pizza bases on a baking sheet and spread with the goat's cheese, then sprinkle with garlic and thyme leaves and top with the artichoke hearts (sliced if they are whole). Scatter the mozzarella and Parmesan cheese over them.

2) Drizzle with olive oil and bake in a very hot oven for 8–10 minutes or until the cheese melts and slightly sizzles. Serve right away.

Aubergine (Eggplant) and Ricotta Pizza

The topping of diced, browned aubergine (eggplant) and light, creamy ricotta is delicious on either a chewy pizza base, thin and delicate flour tortillas or bready focaccio. Choose whichever you favour and is easiest to come by.

SERVES 4

1	medium-sized aubergine (eggplant), cut into bite-sized pieces
several tbsp	extra virgin olive oil, for frying
	salt to taste
4	individual pizza bases, or 8 tortillas or 4 big slices of focaccio
Approximately 400 g/ 14 oz/2⅓ cups	diced tomatoes (tinned is fine)
3 cloves	garlic, chopped
several generous pinches	oregano leaves, crushed
175 g/6 oz	ricotta cheese
4–6 tbsp	freshly grated Parmesan

1) Brown the aubergine (eggplant) in the olive oil in a heavy frying pan, taking care that the aubergine (eggplant) doesn't break up into a mush as you cook it but browns evenly; this should take about 10 minutes. Remove from the heat and salt to taste.
2) Preheat the oven to 200°C/400°F/gas mark 6.
3) Spread each pizza base, tortilla or focaccio with diced tomatoes then sprinkle with garlic and oregano. Spoon the aubergine (eggplant) onto the pizzas, then add dollops of ricotta cheese and sprinkle it all generously with Parmesan.
4) Bake for 10–15 minutes or until the cheese melts and turns golden. Eat right away.

Spicy Courgette (Zucchini) and Green Pepper Pizza

To make this pizza suitable for vegans, omit the sprinkling of cheese at the end.

SERVES 4

4–6	small-to-medium-sized courgettes (zucchini), thinly sliced
1	medium-sized onion, chopped or thinly sliced
5 cloves	garlic, thinly sliced
1	green pepper, diced
3 tbsp	extra virgin olive oil
	salt and freshly ground black pepper to taste
½	hot red pepper or chilli, chopped or dried hot pepper, to taste
400 g/14 oz/2⅓ cups	diced tomatoes (tinned is fine; if using fresh, add 2 tbsp tomato purée to the fresh tomatoes)
pinch	of sugar, to taste
handful	of fresh herbs: chopped rosemary, sage, basil, thyme
4	pizza bases
2–3 tbsp	freshly grated Parmesan or pecorino cheese

1) Sauté the courgettes (zucchini) with the onion, garlic and green pepper in the olive oil until the vegetables are softened. Sprinkle with salt, pepper and chilli, then stir in the tomatoes and cook over a medium-high heat for 5–10 minutes.
2) Season with sugar to taste, then taste for salt and pepper. Stir in the herbs.
3) Spoon the courgettes (zucchini) over the pizza bases, then sprinkle with Parmesan and bake for 10–15 minutes. Serve hot.

Caper and Red Onion-Tomato Pizza on Focaccio

Focaccio makes an excellent base for pizza – if it is very thick, cut it into two thinner slices. If you have no focaccio but a good-quality pizza dough base or good crusty country bread, you could use that in its place.

I might serve a bowl of Risi Bisi alla Venetia for the main course (*see Chapter 5, page 124*), or Pan-Grilled Mediterranean Vegetables (*see Chapter 6, page 136*).

SERVES 4

4–5	ripe tomatoes, finely chopped
2–3 tbsp	tomato purée
3 cloves	garlic, chopped
small pinch	of sugar
3 tbsp	capers
	freshly ground black pepper, to taste
1	large piece of focaccio, cut into 4 portions, or 4 individual focaccie
generous pinch	of dried oregano leaves, crumbled
½–1	red onion, very thinly sliced
175–250 g/6–8 oz/1–1½ cups	mozzarella, Edam, fontina or other white cheese, such as Cheddar
2 tbsp	extra virgin olive oil

1) Preheat the oven to 200°C/400°F/gas mark 6.
2) Combine the tomatoes with the tomato purée, garlic, sugar, capers and black pepper to taste.
3) Spread over the focaccio, then sprinkle with the oregano, onion and cheese, then drizzle with the olive oil.
4) Bake for about 10 minutes or just long enough to melt the cheese to a bubbling, lightly browned topping.
5) Eat right away.

Tomato, Basil and Olive Focaccio

The topping melange of tomatoes, olives and cheese, with a hint of basil, melts into a pizza-like mixture, making a marvellous starter or midnight feast.

SERVES 4

4	large portions of focaccio
4	ripe tomatoes, diced
3 cloves	garlic, chopped
250 g/8 oz/2 cups	white cheese (fontina, Edam, Cheddar, etc.), coarsely chopped or diced
10–15	Mediterranean-style black olives, stoned and coarsely diced or quartered
handful	of basil leaves, coarsely chopped
1–2 tsp	extra virgin olive oil

1) Arrange the foccacio on a baking sheet. If it is very thick, slice it in half.
2) Combine the tomatoes with the garlic, cheese, olives and basil and spoon onto the focaccio in an even layer. Drizzle the top with olive oil
3) Grill until the cheese melts and serve right away.

Piadine with Cheese and Rosemary

Piadine are pancake-like flatbreads from northern Italy, eaten with cheese, salad, antipasti etc. The topping for this pizza-like treat is a heady mixture of garlic, fresh and aged cheeses, and lots of fresh rosemary. The topping of rocket leaves adds a fresh punch and crispness to the rich and melty topping.

A big bowl of vegetable-rich Minestrone al Pesto (*see Chapter 3, page 49*) would make a satisfying supper.

SERVES 4

4	flour tortillas
3 cloves	garlic, chopped
2 tbsp	fresh chopped rosemary
125 g/4 oz	feta or other tangy fresh cheese such as goat's cheese
175 g/6 oz/1½ cups fontina,	Edam, Cheddar or other white cheese, grated
4–6 tbsp	freshly grated Parmesan or pecorino cheese
40 g/1½ oz/½ cup	rocket leaves

1) Arrange the tortillas on a baking sheet and preheat the grill.
2) Mix the garlic with the rosemary, feta or goat's cheese, fontina (or Edam or Cheddar), Parmesan or pecorino. Divide into 4 portions and spread evenly on each tortilla.
3) Grill until the cheese melts and turns lightly golden in spots.
4) Serve right away, each one topped with a handful of rocket leaves.

Cheese and Tomato Piadina with Rocket

The combination of cheese and diced tomatoes melts into a tangy garlicky topping, with the rocket adding its pungent freshness as a salady topping.

SERVES 4

4	flour tortillas or piadine
2 cloves	garlic, chopped
175 g/6 oz/1½ cups	shredded mild white cheese such as fontina or Cheddar
a drizzle	of olive oil
1–2	ripe, diced tomatoes
several handfuls	of arugula (rocket) leaves, preferably older, spicier specimens
12–16	green olives, preferably Sicilian ones with a slightly bitter cast

1) Arrange the tortillas on a baking sheet and sprinkle with the garlic, cheese, olive oil and tomatoes. Grill until the cheese melts and the edge of the tortillas are lightly browned.
2) Serve right away, topped with the arugula and olives.

Dolci
Desserts

Italian fruit is so sun-sweet, so fresh and juicy that there is little else one needs to end a meal. Rich sweets and cakes can come at another time, say with an espresso in the afternoon, or with a glass of grappa in the evening.

Sometimes the fruit is embellished, as in the following quickly made desserts, and sometimes a little of Italy's superb ice cream – *gelato* – is too hard to resist.

Cocomero

This dish of watermelon with lime is courtesy of Kamala Friedman, who fed it to me on her tree-shaded terrace one sultry summer evening after a feast of gnocchi and artichokes.

SERVES 4

1 watermelon, rind and seeds removed, cut into bite-sized chunks
juice of ½–1 lime
grated zest of ½ lime
sugar to taste (as needed)

1) Toss the watermelon chunks with the lime juice, lemon zest and sugar. Eat right away or chill until ready to eat.

Figs with Raspberries and Anice

SERVES 4

12–16 ripe figs, sliced lengthways

1 punnet raspberries

several tbsp anise-flavoured liqueur such as Anice,
Anisette or Sambuca
raspberry sorbet (optional)

1) Arrange the figs on a plate. Garnish with raspberries and drizzle with Anice, Anisette or Sambuca. Serve as is, or with a small scoop of raspberry sorbet in the middle.

Variation

This can also be made by lightly cooking the figs, as the heat of the fire intensifies their sweet flavour. Brush the halved figs with a little honey or sprinkle them with sugar, drizzle them with the anise liqueur, then warm them on the barbecue or grill, or roast them for about 10 minutes in the oven. Serve warm or cool.

Pomegranates with Liqueurs

This recipe is sheer simplicity: bring sweet pomegranates to the table with a few embellishments and let each person concoct his or her own dessert. If you require a bit more of a polished dessert, take the seeds out of the pomegranate before serving, splash it with the liqueur and Cognac, and toss with sugar to taste. Other exotic fruit, such as lychees, mango and kiwi, can be added to this bowl, reducing the number of pomegranates to 2.

SERVES 4

4 pomegranates
a bottle of Grand Marnier or Cointreau
a bottle of Cognac
sugar, to taste

1) Bring to the table a bowl of pomegranates and a bottle of Grand Marnier and Cognac, and let each eater open his or her pomegranate and dress it with the liqueur and Cognac, adding sugar to taste.

Strawberries and Balsamic Vinegar

Balsamic vinegar brings out the brightness of the berries – be sure you only add a drop or two though, or you might end up with strawberry vinaigrette. Lightly whipped cream – *panna*, in Italy – is always delicious on tangy, fresh berries; so is frozen or Greek yoghurt.

SERVES 4

1 punnet strawberries, cleaned and halved
a few drops of balsamic vinegar
sugar, to taste

1) Combine the strawberries with the balsamic and sugar. Eat right away or chill.

Raspberries with White Chocolate Fondue

Deliciously indulgent. Either serve the raspberries in a bowl with the molten white chocolate for dipping, or spoon the sauce over and around the berries on plates. A good-quality sponge cake on the side in little pieces makes a delicious balance for the rich sauce and tangy, fresh berries.

SERVES 4

250 g/8 oz/1½ cups	white chocolate
90 ml/3 fl oz/⅓ cup	double cream
2 tbsp	fruit brandy or eau di vie
1 punnet	raspberries

1) Break or cut the white chocolate into small chunks. Process in a food processor until they are the size and shape of coarse grains. This will help the chocolate melt more easily – if you don't have a processor, just cut them into smallish chunks with a knife.

2) Gently heat the cream and chocolate together in a double boiler until the chocolate melts, then stir in the fruit brandy or eau de vie and a little more cream if needed for a smooth consistency.

3) Serve with the berries.

Pear Tart

A thin layer of caramelized pears lies on top of an almondy paste that absorbs the juices of the pears and keeps the tart light rather than sodden, as can happen with deliciously juicy fruit.

This tart is simple to make, impressive to serve and, most importantly, it is luscious to eat. It can be made in a round pan but I like the rustic charm of a free-form tart baked on a flat baking sheet.

SERVES ABOUT 6–8

500 g/1 lb	puff pastry (purchased)
90–125 g/6–8 oz/1–1½ cups	ground almonds (almond meal)
8–10 tbsp	sugar, or as desired
⅛–¼ tsp	almond essence, or as desired
4–6	pears, ripe but firm, peeled, cored and sliced thinly
3–4 tbsp	butter

1) Roll out the pastry until it is about 3 mm (⅛ in) thick. Sprinkle it with the almonds, leaving a border around the edge, then sprinkle with the most of the sugar (saving 2–3 tbsp for sprinkling over the pears) and with the almond essence. Make a layer of the pears, then fold up the edges of the pastry to enclose the tart. Sprinkle the top of the pears with the sugar and almond essence then dot with the butter and bake at 190°C/375°F/gas mark 5 for 15–20 minutes or long enough to bake the pastry and cook through and caramelize the pears.

Grilled Peaches with Ripe Blackberries

The combination of rich grilled peaches with light fresh berries is
fine indeed.

SERVES 4

4 peaches or nectarines, halved and stoned
sugar for sprinkling
butter for dotting over the fruit
brandy for sprinkling (optional)

1 punnet blackberries

1) Arrange the peaches or nectarines cut side up on a baking
   sheet and sprinkle with sugar, dot with butter and drizzle
   with brandy.
2) Grill or bake in a hot oven until the peaches are slightly
   browned in spots, just growing tender and lightly glazed.
3) Remove from the heat and serve sprinkled with the blackberries (tossed with a little of the sugar and brandy if desired).
   Accompany with pistachio ice cream, if desired, for a dish as
   beautiful as it is delicious: pale-green ice cream, roasty peach-
   coloured fruit, nuggets of purple blackberries.

Gooey Grilled Pineapple

This looks very appealing garnished with a scattering of pistachio nuts (be sure they are unsalted and raw) and thin strands of the zest of an orange, but it tastes just as delicious unadorned. Serve with slices of pannetone, a lovely but not too sweet yeast cake from Piedmont, usually purchased rather than homemade, and a tiny scoop of vanilla or pistachio ice cream.

This recipe is good hot, but equally tasty cooled to room temperature, something like the gooey topping of a pineapple upside-down cake.

SERVES 4

1 ripe pineapple
2–3 tbsp butter
light brown sugar or demerara, as desired

1) Peel the pineapple and slice. Remove or leave the core, as you desire. Arrange the pineapple on a baking sheet and dot or spread with the butter, then coat with the sugar. Grill under a medium-low heat until the sugar caramelizes, then turn over and do the same on the other side. You want the pineapple to be just cooked through and the sugar caramelized.

Amaretti-baked Apricots

Amaretti means 'just a tiny bit bitter', and so describes the distinctive bitter-almond flavour of this sweet little biscuit.

Amaretti were invented in the early 1700s in Saronno, Italy, by a young baker who created them for a visiting cardinal, and wound up winning the hand of the woman he loved. It was her idea to wrap the biscuits in the pastel-coloured papers, and the descendants of that baker and his wife still make the biscuits today.

SERVES 4

12	ripe sweet apricots, halved and stoned
8	amaretti, roughly broken up
1–2 tbsp	caster sugar
	vanilla ice cream

1) Preheat the oven to 200°C/400°F/gas mark 6.
2) Arrange the apricots in a shallow baking dish then sprinkle with the amaretti and sugar on top. Cover tightly with foil.
3) Bake for 15–20 minutes or until the apricots and amaretti are a sweet, fragrant, messy mixture.
4) Serve each portion with a scoop of ice cream.

Gelato con Sambuca

This takes the classic combination of Sambuca and coffee to a frozen pudding.

SERVES 4

6–8	dark roast coffee beans
570 ml/1 pint (for polite people) or 1 litre/2 pints (for greedy people)	good-quality coffee or vanilla ice cream
90–140 ml/3–5 fl oz/⅓–⅔ cup	Sambuca

1) Lightly crush the coffee beans with a pestle and mortar or between sheets of wax paper or parchment with a rolling pin.
2) Serve scoops of the ice cream drizzled with Sambuca to taste and sprinkled with crushed coffee beans.

Frozen Cappuccino

SERVES 2 GREEDY PEOPLE AS A

SNACK-MEAL OR 4 PEOPLE AS DESSERT

250 ml/8 fl oz/1 cup milk (I use semi-skimmed)

2 shots of espresso, or strong filter coffee, cooled

4 scoops (about 570 ml/1 pint) ice cream – choose vanilla, chocolate, coffee or hazelnut

1–2 shots of any alcohol in a compatible flavour: amaretto, Tia Maria, etc. (optional)

1) Place all ingredients in a blender and whirl. Drink or spoon right away.

Chocolate Ice Cream Truffles

This is basically a scoop of dark chocolate ice cream rolled in shaved chocolate, then stuck in the freezer to settle a bit while you eat dinner. Serve it with a splash of rum, if you like, or a drift of snowy whipped cream.

SERVES 4

570 ml/1 pint   good-quality chocolate ice cream

175–200 g/6–7 oz/1 cup   plain chocolate, shaved

to serve: a few tbsp   of rum, and lightly whipped cream, as desired

1) Scoop the chocolate into 4, 8 or 12 balls, depending on the size of your scooper. Roll each scoop in shaved plain chocolate then place on a clingfilm-lined baking sheet and freeze while you eat the rest of the meal. If you wish to leave these in the freezer for longer, for days or even weeks, wrap the tray in clingfilm to protect them against the drying effect of the freezer.

2) Serve each portion with a drizzle of rum, if desired, and a dollop of whipped cream. Eat right away.

Resources

The following shops sell an exhilarating selection of Italian products. Many supermarkets do too, such as Marks and Spencer's delicious Italian baked goods and *biscotti*. There are numerous delis throughout London and the country that stock wonderful, delicious Italian products.

Harvey Nichols Foodshop
5th Floor
Knightsbridge
London SW1
Tel. 0171–235 5000

Carluccio's
28a Neal Street
London WC2
Tel. 0171–240 1487

Fortnum and Mason
181 Piccadilly
London W1
Tel. 0171–734 8040
Fax 0171–437 3278

Foxes of Wandsworth
14 Bellevue Road
London SW17
Tel. 0181–672 0987

Gazzano and Son
167 Farringdon Road
London EC1
Tel. 0171–837 1586

Selfridges
400 Oxford Street
London W1
Tel. 0171–629 1234

Thomas and Thomas
Tel. 0171–729 6006

For mail-order dried mushrooms. In addition to a wide range of dried mushrooms (from France, but the ceps taste Italian), they also sell a powdered porcini for sprinkling over risotti, etc.

G. Rowe Mushroom Sales Ltd.
Stand 46, Borough Market
London SE1
Tel. 0171–407 9051

Geoff Rowe is 'The Mushroom Man'. If you have a chance, there is nothing more Italian than fresh mushroom pasta or risotto, and Geoff is your man with the mushrooms.

The Conran Shop
Michelin House
81 Fulham Road
London SW3
Tel. 0171–589 7401

Gianni Parmigiani
Parmigiani and Lawrence
Importers Ltd.
6 Old Ford Trading Centre
Maverton Road
London E3 2JE
Tel. 0181–980 3333
Fax 0181–981 3450

Fantastico Parmigiana cheese, olive oil, and a wide array of various pickled and marinated delicacies; their hot red chilli paste is superb.

Grania and Sarnia
6 Sterne St
London W12 8AD
Tel. 0181–749 8274

Exceptional olive oils, quail egg pasta, and truffle/porcini paste to die for.

John Burgess Exports
No. 1 Harley St
London W1N 1DA
Tel. 0171–637 1828
Fax 0171–636 8789

Italian olive oils.
Odysea
2/3 Charterhouse Square
London EC1M 6EE
Tel. 0171–251 0404
Fax 0171–251 1986

Importers of olives, olive oils, saffron and Mediterranean food products

Vivian's
2 Worple Way
Richmond
Surrey
Tel. 0181–940 3600

Valvona and Crolla
19 Elm Row
Edinburgh

Fratelli Sarti
133 Wellington Street
Glasgow

Index

Of further interest…

30 Minute Vegetarian Indian Cookbook

Mridula Baljekar

Indian dishes have a reputation of being time-consuming and complicated. But they don't have to be – Mridula Baljekar's quick and easy recipes enable you to prepare and serve delicious and authentic Indian meals in 30 minutes.

Mridula Baljekar has adapted many traditional Indian dishes especially for vegetarians including inspirational curries, spicy vegetable dishes, fragrant rice and dhal.

Mridula Baljekar is a successful Indian cookery writer and TV broadcaster. She is author of Mridula Baljekar's Real Balti Cookbook, Vegetarian Balti Cooking, A Taste of Goa and The Complete Indian Cookbook.

ISBN: 0 7225 3410 8

30 Minute Vegetarian Mexican Cookbook

Sarah Beattie

Mexican food has never been so simple. Refreshing gazpacho for hot summer days, fiery salsa, crispy tostada, baked burritos, indulgent enchiladas[el]and all made with the freshest of vegetarian foods.

Sarah Beattie has adapted many traditional Mexican recipes, using ingredients such as hot and mellow chillies, the sharp flavours of limes and tomatoes; the cool taste of avocado, coriander and sour cream; and a rich variety of beans and cheeses. In a half hour you can create delicious soups, main courses and desserts to give you the unique taste of Mexico.

Sarah Beattie is a successful vegetarian cookery author and TV broadcaster. She has written 30 Minute Thai Cookbook, Neither Fish Nor Fowl – Meatfree Eating for Pleasure, and Table of Content – A Vegetarian Dinner Party Book for All Seasons.

ISBN: 0 7225 3426 4

30 Minute Vegetarian Thai Cookbook

Sarah Beattie

Thai food has never been so simple. Using ingredients such as hot chillies, cooling coconut, limes, ginger, lemongrass and aromatic herbs you can discover how to make tasty Thai curries, spicy salads and soups, ready to serve in 30 minutes or less.

Sarah Beattie has adapted many traditional Thai recipes, using mostly fresh foods, combining sweet, salty, sour and spicy to give you the unique taste of Thailand.

ISBN: 0 7225 3425 6

30 Minute Vegetarian Turkish Cookbook

Sarah Beattie

Turkey is a place where East meets West and its cuisine is one of rich contrasts: from the exotic richness of the Ottoman Empire to the simplicity of Mediterranean peasant food. Colourful salads, Turkish pizza (pide) and pasta, a delicious array of meze dishes, comforting soups and casseroles, dolmas and kebabs, crisp pastries and sweet puddings have been made simple to prepare and ready to serve in 30 minutes.

ISBN: 0 7225 3624 0

Food From the Place

Bill Sewell

In 1989 Bill Sewell opened The Place Below restaurant in the Norman crypt of St Mary-le-Bow church in the heart of the City of London. It is considered by many to be the best vegetarian restaurant in the capital.

> 'Bill Sewell belongs to the new generation of vegetarian food writers. There's nothing puritanical or worthily dull about his kind of food. It is as vibrant and appetising as all good food should be'
>
> *Sophie Grigson*

ISBN: 0 7225 3230 X

Cheap and Easy
Vegetarian Cooking on a Budget

Rose Elliot

Fast, full of flavour and totally delicious, this carefully selected range of vegetarian recipes have been created with economy in mind, but never at the expense of taste and variety.

Chapters include wonderful meals with vegetables, cheese, eggs, pies, nuts and pluses, as well as a tempting array of puddings, cakes and biscuits.

Every recipe is calorie-counted and uses fresh, nutritious ingredients, making this the perfect cookbook for anyone who values good cooking as well as good health.

ISBN: 0 7225 3117 6

Vegetarian Four Seasons

Rose Elliot

Vegetarian Four Seasons takes you on a culinary journey through the year, with a specially-chosen collection of delicious recipes. Fresh, clean tastes in spring; soothing flavours for hot summer days; mellow, rich dishes for autumn; and warming, hearty food to help keep out the winter cold.

This collection of seasonal recipes includes wild mushroom ragoût, roasted winter vegetables with lemon and horseradish, pasta primavera and sunny asparagus. Rose Elliot also includes useful menus to help you plan special occasions.

ISBN: 0 7225 3361 6

Not Just a Load of Old Lentils
The Ideal Introduction to Vegetarian Cooking

Rose Elliot

Rose Elliot's classic introduction to vegetarian cookery has been widely praised as one of the very best vegetarian wholefood cookery books ever written. From starters and salads to main meals, gateaux and desserts, she expands the basic vegetarian kitchen to include the colours and versatility of pulse-based meals using beans and lentils, savoury meat substitutes and a wealth of other vegetarian flavours. Special features include: a nutritional guide for vegetarians, a seasonal menu planner, recipes for slimmers, party themes and a clear glossary of foods.

ISBN: 0 7225 3037 4